M

P

An Illustrated History

ILLUSTRATED HISTORIES FROM HIPPOCRENE

Published…

Arizona
Patrick Lavin

Celtic World
Patrick Lavin

China
Yong Ho

Cracow
Zdzislaw Zygulski

England
Henry Weisser

France
Lisa Neal

Greece
Tom Stone

Ireland
Henry Weisser

Israel
David C. Gross

Italy
Joseph F. Privitera

Korea
David Rees

Mexico
Michael Burke

Paris
Elaine Mokhtefi

Poland
Iwo Cyprian Pogonowski

Poland in World War II
Andrew Hempel

Russia
Joel Carmichael

Spain
Fred James Hill

Tikal
John Montgomery

Forthcoming…

Egypt
Fred James Hill

Gypsy World
Atanas Slavov

London
Nick Awde & Robert Chester

Moscow
Kathy Murrell

Portugal
Lisa Neal

Romania
Nicholas Klepper

Sicily
Joseph F. Privitera

Venice
Lisa Neal

Vietnam
Shelton Woods

Wales
Henry Weisser

PARIS

An Illustrated History

Elaine Mokhtefi

HIPPOCRENE BOOKS, INC.
New York

ISBN 0–7818–0838–3

For information, address:
HIPPOCRENE BOOKS, INC.
171 Madison Avenue
New York, NY 10016
www.hippocrenebooks.com

Cataloging–in–Publication data available from the Library of Congress.

Printed in the United States of America.

TABLE OF CONTENTS

INTRODUCTION

Paris is an old city molded by time. Obviously, it is not a planned city: no Washington or New York. Events and history have shaped Paris, with the hands of the men and women who have fashioned it evident everywhere. The city has benefited from an outstanding geographical position at the juncture of five rivers, one of which, the Seine, links it to the sea. It is tempered by the Gulf Stream and surrounded by rich agricultural lands that are easily exploitable. In the centuries preceding our era, it was part of the chain of transport and commercial activity that joined northern Europe to the Mediterranean and Eastern Europe. Later, it became the leading city of the land that would become France, and then its capital. By the Middle Ages, Paris was recognized as a beacon of opportunity and attracted the best in artisans and workers. The city's university was unrivaled, its architecture admired and copied throughout Europe. Its conversion from a medieval to a Renaissance city in the 16th and 17th centuries was evidence of its capacity for change, its willingness to open itself to new concepts and design. At the end of the 18th century, it became the crucible of one of the most significant revolutions in history. Its artists, writers, and philosophers from the 18th century onward have had universal appeal and have conferred upon the city an aura of intelligence, taste, and style that is incomparable. Indeed, for many, Paris is the most beautiful city in the world.

CHAPTER 1

FROM SIMPLE BEGINNINGS

THE CELTS

At the confluence of Paris' five rivers, a number of small islands once jutted upward out of swampy waters. It was amidst the natural protection of these waterlogged bits of land that the first Parisians settled. In order to gain the shores of the mainland, these inhabitants island-hopped. A bow, tools, and dugout canoes uncovered during excavations in the early 1990s attest to the fact that human settlements have survived continuously at this location for 6,000 years.

By the Bronze Age (1800 to 700 B.C.), the Seine had already become a major commercial waterway for metals mined in England and transported to the Mediterranean and Eastern Europe. A Celtic population arrived in the region during the Second Iron Age, probably in the 3rd century B.C. The Celts were horsemen who wielded iron swords and lived nomadic lives until they settled in the region. There is little doubt that they mixed with an earlier population, known as the Danubians, who resided along the Seine and engaged in river trading.

Little is known of the Celts, yet many historians confer upon them the prestige awarded to founders of a nation. Ascribed to

1

them are traits of character such as strength, courage, and resistance, which are considered to be at the heart of the French nation. However, they are also depicted as illiterate and bellicose.

In any case, their mark on society was decidedly less enduring than that of the Romans, who would introduce the Latin language (which gradually evolved into French), the first schools, city planning, and architectural achievements such as multi-storied buildings, the induction of water by aqueduct, stone-cutting, and masonry.

The first historical mention of Paris was, in fact, inscribed by Julius Caesar in *De Bello Gallico*. He signaled the existence of a people called the Parisii and an *oppidum*—a structure similar to a fort that generally contained a market—called Lutetia, which was situated on an island in the Seine. The Parisii most likely lived in low, round, thatched-roof huts that were made of mud, wood, or simple adobe, and that stood along the river banks or close to the *oppidum*. The island upon which the Parisii resided, Ile de la Cité, today sustains Sainte-Chapelle, Notre-Dame de Paris, the Conciergerie, and the Justice Courts.

The Parisii Celts were part of Gaul. For several centuries the Gauls had pillaged throughout Europe, even managing to sack Rome in 390 B.C. When Julius Caesar marched north to capture Gaul in 58 B.C., however, they were in decline and threatened by both the Teutons and the Romans. Caesar's army was small and determined, while the Gauls were ill-organized and feuding.

Asterix, a popular children's comic-book character, represents the petit but clever and courageous embodiment of France's Gallic ancestors.

The Roman Conquest

The Roman conquest became final in 52 B.C., when Vercingetorix, who had succeeded in uniting the Gauls, was defeated at Alesia. Caesar, always imperial, referred to the defeated people as "rabble."

Romanization took: by the middle of the 1st century A.D., the rude *oppidum* of Lutetia had been transformed into a Roman town. From the island, it expanded to the left bank of the Seine. Its main axis was north-south along the Rue Saint-Jacques; its center, the Forum, was situated under present-day Rue Soufflot, between Rue Saint-Jacques and Boulevard Saint-Michel. Three baths served the city, the largest being those at Cluny, vestiges of which are part of the Cluny Museum. Water was carried by aqueduct for ten miles to source them. On Rue Monge exist the remains of an amphitheater, the Lutetia Arena (Arènes de Lutèce), which was built to hold 15,000 people despite the fact that the population at the time was probably under 6,000.

The 3rd century saw the decline of the little town on the Seine. New Germanic invaders arrived from the East—the Alamans and the Franks. The city was laid to waste, pillaged, and its population was decimated. Survivors constructed a rampart around the Ile de la Cité and holed up within its confines. The left bank became the seat of the Roman armies in Gaul. Towards the end of the century, the city took the name of its inhabitants: Paris.

Thermes de Cluny. Dating from 200 A.D., the Roman baths at Cluny were equipped with a frigidarium and a pool, still recognizable at the Cluny Museum.

Built in the 1ˢᵗ century A.D., the Lutetia Arena was rediscovered during excavations in 1869. Today, soccer-playing teenagers occupy the field on which gladiators once battled to the death.

CHRISTIANITY

Saint Dennis, the first bishop of Paris, arrived from Italy in about 250 A.D., his mission being to teach the Gospel to the recalcitrant Gauls. Castigated for his beliefs, he was decapitated at the top of Montmartre—Mount of the Martyr. According to legend, he tucked his head under his arm and trudged off to the place now called Saint-Denis, where the cathedral that houses the tombs of French kings is found.

Though the first Christian church was built in the 4th century, it was a woman's piety and courage that produced Christianity's most significant advances. Faced with the arrival of Attila and the Huns c. 450, the population of the island readied itself to flee; but Geneviève, a Christian shepherdess who would later become the patron saint of Paris, convinced the inhabitants to hold their ground in prayer. The Huns simply passed by the city.

In 464, Franks under the command of Childeric attacked and blockaded the island city. Geneviève again came to the rescue, bringing in supplies by water. However, a subsequent decade-long blockade by the Franks took enough of a toll to bring her to the negotiating table. For Paris, this event spelled the end of Roman rule.

Kneeling in the Woods, *by Puvis de Chavannes.*
Part of a series of the life of Saint Genevieve, it
hangs in the Pantheon, originally the Church of
Sainte-Geneviève.

CHAPTER 2

THROUGH THE DARK AGES

Capital of the Franks

The Frankish monarchs—the first series of whom were known as Merovingians and the second series as Carolingians—would rule well into the 10th century, a period of six centuries that remains relatively obscure. In 508 Paris was chosen as the royal capital by Clovis (r. 481–511), a recent convert to Catholicism. Under the Merovingians, fourteen churches were built for a population of roughly 20,000. Church councils that assembled metropolitans (archbishops) and bishops were also convened in the city.

The Ile de la Cité was the center of town. The existence of several ports on the Seine and the presence of Jewish and Syrian traders attest to the extent of water commerce. Members of the royal Merovingian family fought each other for control of the city, passing sections of it back and forth among themselves and treating it like a family estate. By the end of the 7th century, the Frankish kings had become considerably weakened—degenerate, according to some accounts. They became, in fact, itinerant monarchs who drifted from one to another of their countryside properties, devouring local goods and produce. History refers to them as the *rois fainéants*, or the do-nothing kings.

SAINT·GERMAIN·DES·PRES ·PARIS·

St. Germain-des-Prés. When Childebert, son of Clovis, returned from battle in Spain with relics of an early Spanish martyr, he built the Church of St. Germain-des-Prés to house his booty. The present church contains little of the 6th-century structure, reduced to ruins by Norman invaders some 300 years later.

The Carolingians

Pépin the Short, Charlemagne's father, defeated the *rois fainéants* in battle in 751. There then emerged a new line of Frankish monarchs who would be known as the Carolingians. The most illustrious of these kings was Charlemagne (r. 768–814), who was to become the sovereign head of the Frankish Empire and then of the Holy Roman Empire.

Charlemagne did not reside in Paris. He created his capital at Aix-la-Chapelle (Aachen, Germany), from which city he ruled over an area that extended from Eastern Europe to the Atlantic and northern Spain. Even Rome owed him allegiance, and an indebted Pope Leo III declared him Emperor of the Romans "crowned by God." Charlemagne died in 814, just as his realm was being subjected to the first incursions of a new set of invaders, the Norse or Vikings.

To this day, Charlemagne remains a legendary figure in the manner of Caesar or Napoleon. His statue stands in the square in front of Notre-Dame, depicting a bearded giant of a man. Unfortunately, it bears little resemblance to the tubby, stooped, clean-shaven person he was in life.

Charlemagne's successors were weak and ineffectual. They divided and re-divided the extensive lands amongst themselves and their offspring. They even went to war with each other. (Charlemagne's immediate successor died in battle against his own son.) These were the darkest of the Dark Ages, years of anarchy, corruption, and the exercise of raw power.

In the middle of the 9th century, however, three of Charlemagne's grandsons finally concluded a treaty that bound each of them to a different section of the Empire. These territories correspond roughly to modern-day Germany (eastern kingdom);

modern-day France (western kingdom); and the northern territories of Belgium and the Netherlands (middle kingdom). The area of Lorraine (France), which originally formed part of the middle kingdom, would be at stake between the two European powers well into the 20th century.

The statue of Charlemagne in the foreground of Notre-Dame was erected at the end of the 19th century. It was part of a group of 124 statues inaugurated by the Third Republic in a city hitherto largely devoid of statuary

The Normans

The first Parisian incursion of Norse invaders occurred in 845. They arrived from Norway and Denmark in small, maneuverable boats called *drakkars* (dragons), which were capable of navigating inland waterways. They pillaged Paris and demanded a heavy ransom in exchange for their departure later that year.

Some ten years later, however, they returned and burned most of the churches to the ground, while ransoming those that were left standing. Norse incursions became regular, harrowing events until 889 when an attack on Paris was finally resisted. They continued to ravage other parts of France until 911, at which time they were awarded the dukedom of Normandy and were thus appeased.

During the reign of the Carolingians, Paris was governed by a series of counts. At first named by the king and usually members of the royal family, the title became hereditary with the successors of Robert the Strong, called the Robertinians. One such count, Eudes son of Robert, had distinguished himself during the Norman invasion of 885. The invaders had arrived on 700 ships and demanded passage along the Seine. Their request refused, they initiated a siege that lasted a full year. After displaying his mettle in battle, Eudes succeeded in slipping out of the city and reaching the emperor. Though Charles the Fat subsequently arrived at the head of an army, he did not fight but rather negotiated with the attackers, bribing them with silver and license to extend their pillage into Burgundy. Since Frankish kings of this time were, as a general rule, elected by their peers, Charles was deposed in the wake of this event and Eudes chosen to govern in 888.

For another century, descendants of the Robertinians held power over a territory that extended from the Seine to the Loire.

Between 845 and 911, drakkars served the Norsemen for their incursions along the coast and on the inland waterways of France. Thirty thousand Norse sailor-soldiers aboard 700 drakkars took part in the siege of Paris in 885.

In 987 a Robertinian descendant, Hugh Capet (r. 987–996), was crowned king of France; he was the first in a new line of regents, the Capetians. Their power originated with the Catholic Church and depended largely on an entente with it for survival.

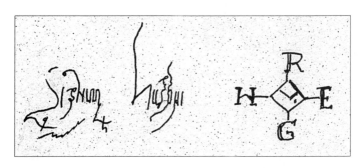

Hugues Capet's signature, reproduced from a diploma delivered in 989. The writing on the left "Signum Hugoni" (Hugues' signature) is followed by a mixture of the words "Hugo" and "rex" (king) in the shape of a cross.

CHAPTER 3

CITY AND CAPITAL

THE CAPETIANS

For centuries, Paris had remained one city among many in France. With the division of Charlemagne's territory into three parts, however, it was no longer peripheral and the city gradually gained in importance. Robert the Pious, a Capetian who ruled from 996 to 1031, spent considerable time there. He restored the Conciergerie and several churches, among them Saint-Germain-des-Prés, which had served as a garrison for the Normans during the invasion of 885–886.

Under Philip I (r. 1060–1108), ecclesiastics became the largest landowners of the city. The land holdings of the powerful and wealthy Saint-Germain Abbey, for example, reached all around the city. While the Ile de la Cité still constituted the center of Paris, small settlements were emerging on the left and right banks, especially in the immediate vicinity of churches. The fame of certain of them, such as Saint-Germain-des-Prés attracted waves of pilgrims from around the country.

By the 12th century, Paris had outclassed Orleans as the key city of the realm. When King Philip Augustus departed for the crusades in 1190, the two principal organs of government, Justice and the Treasury, were housed in Paris. The Saint-Denis Abbey had become the leading monastery and the place where kings were entombed. The left bank or University—actually numerous varied buildings in which teachers and their disciples gathered—attracted students from near and afar.

The 12th century saw economic activity in Paris reach new heights. The association of water merchants or traders obtained a monopoly over all traffic by water; its jurisdiction was gradually extended to include, among other domains, matters of justice involving trade. The authority exercised by them would be the embryo of municipal administration.

A new market (later to become Les Halles) and a new port were also built during this time, thereby according commercial preeminence to the right bank. The Temple was also founded on the right bank during this period, and housed the Order of the Knights Templar; while churches on the left bank gave rise to the communities of Saint-Germain-des-Prés, Saint-Marcel, Sainte-Geneviève, and Saint-Médard. The left bank remained essentially rural, however, and these hamlets were separated by fields and orchards. The land had been cleared for cultivation, thereby making it ready for the next step, urbanization.

A direct line of Capetians would remain in power for 350 years. France owes to them the timid beginnings of the state, the first since the demise of the administration put in place by the Romans more than a millennium earlier. While the political and economic weight of the ecclesiastics was considerable, royalty maintained numerous properties within the city limits and throughout the country, as well as privileges that extended their power and supported an opulent lifestyle.

Like most medieval towns, Paris had been a market town whose primary economic activity stemmed from the need to feed its citizens. The wealth of the royal family, of the nobility and of a certain elite; the quartering of the military; the creation of governing agencies; and the arrival of immigrants from the countryside and abroad created new demands that were gradually satisfied by a new class of craftspeople and merchants. As the population expanded, so did its needs for goods, housing, space, and organization. Paris could now lay claim to attributes of a real city, at last mirroring those of the great metropolises of the Arab world—Damascus, Qayrawan, and Baghdad.

PHILIP AUGUSTUS

King Philip II (r. 1180–1223), or Philip Augustus, chose Paris as his residence, maintaining two domiciles: the Conciergerie on the Ile de la Cité, and Vincennes. He was instrumental in making it the permanent capital of France, and encouraged the transformation of rural Paris into a city of commerce and crafts. Vibrant growth made the city a pole of attraction for people throughout the realm. In addition to nobles and soldiers, artisans and laborers of all sorts pressed into the city. The list of trades to be found in the narrow streets and back alleys was exhaustive and ever-increasing. Rules governing these professions were elaborated. The fortune of the monarchy depended on the development of the economy.

One of Philip's first acts, in 1182, was the expulsion of the Jews from the city and the confiscation of their businesses and estates, which were considerable since they were prominent in money-lending and numerous trades. The subsequent benefits for the monarchy went beyond simple acquisition, for a new class of merchants and traders could be gratified with the takings. The result of this economic activity was the birth of a bourgeoisie to whom the king entrusted the affairs of the city upon his departure for the crusades in 1189. In doing so, he bypassed members of the nobility for the most essential of these tasks, including that of the city's accounts.

Philip Augustus had certain of the main thoroughfares of the city paved. The Roman pavements had long been buried under layers of dirt and garbage, and walking the muddy, rotten streets had become a perilous endeavor. Fearing problems with his Norman and English neighbors, he gave orders to build a fortified wall around the city. Construction lasted thirty-five years. The wall was eight to twelve feet wide, some thirty feet high, and it enclosed not only the immediate city but its outlying districts, thereby readying Paris for surges of expansion. In 1202 the Louvre donjon was completed. Placed on the edge of the right bank, this donjon or citadel, was to be the first edifice of the future Louvre Palace. Here, Philip Augustus interred prisoners of note, arms, documents, and his treasure of ingots, money, and jewels.

Commenced under his father in 1163, the cathedral of Notre-Dame also rose from the ground during Philip's reign. (It would be completed one century later, while Saint-Louis held the throne.) The new Gothic architecture practiced in a small way at the Saint-Denis Abbey and more decisively at Notre-Dame has given its title to the period itself: the Gothic Era, the significance of this term being not only architectural but societal, in that it evokes the feudal system that characterized medieval France.

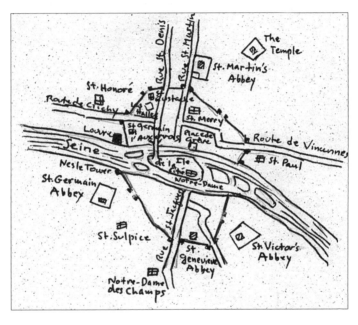

Map of Paris, after a map produced in the beginning of the 13th century. It includes the wall built under Philip Augustus.

SAINT LOUIS

The grandson of Philip Augustus, Louis IX or Saint Louis (r. 1226–1270), has entered the historical record as an uncompromising religious fanatic beloved by his people. Early in his reign, he learned that the "true crown of thorns" was for sale in Constantinople. The price was high and many doubted its authenticity, but Saint Louis would not be dissuaded. When it arrived in France, the Very Christian King (as he was called) and his brothers carried it, barefoot, along an itinerary of some seventy miles to Notre-Dame. There it awaited the Sainte-Chapelle, designed by Pierre de Montreuil and completed in 1248.

His faith also led him to strengthen restrictions against Jews and to pursue avidly the inquisition of Muslims, known at the time simply as "the infidels." So-called heretics were blinded and burned. In his role as a soldier of Christ, he sought to deliver the Holy Land from the Muslims and, in 1248, led an expedition aimed at capturing Jerusalem and bringing Christ's tomb to France. Taken prisoner, he remained in the East for four more years. It was during his second crusade, in 1271, that he was fatally stricken during the plague.

In Saint Louis, however, the poor had a champion. Although he saw no need to question the feudal system, he wished it humanized. Towards this end he demanded more honesty in commerce and banished usurers; codified the rules for the exercise of crafts and commerce; introduced new gold and silver coins; and stopped the emissions of monies by feudal lords. Saint Louis also rendered justice in a more personal fashion . . . under the oaks at Vincennes. Because of their allegiance to their faith, certain historians compare Saint Louis to Joan of Arc.

Sainte-Chapelle. The chapel has two levels: a lower level intended for royal servants, and an upper level for the monarch, his family, and the relics for which Sainte-Chapelle was built. Two-thirds of the exceptional stained glass windows are originals.

Notre-Dame Cathedral. The cathedral was badly mutilated following the Revolution, but was restored to its present state beginning in 1845. The name of the original architect is unknown; the restoration, however, was undertaken by architects Eugene Viollet-le-Duc and Jean-Baptiste-Antoine Lassus.

CHAPTER 4

WAR AND CONFLICT

Inglorious Times

Divine right had been invoked by the Capetians as they passed the crown of France from one head to the next. Those who succeeded Saint Louis, however, left far lesser marks. Financial demands on the population were constant and insistent. New monies were needed to satisfy an increasingly exigent royal house; to recruit and sustain armies and expeditions; to satisfy an expanding and ghoulish bureaucracy; and to finance the marriage of the monarch's daughters and the equipment of his sons. The means employed to raise these needed funds were the usual—taxation, devaluation, and, on occasion, revaluation—as well as confiscation and dispossession. In the early 14th century, Philip the Fair (r. 1285–1314) revaluated French currency, producing rent increases of 200 to 300 percent; Paris rebelled against its landlords. The leaders of the uprising were hung from elms at the gates of the city.

The relationship between the monarchy and the bourgeoisie, which had been bonded and sealed over time, was also put to the test during the 14th century. The Black Plague and the endless war with the English, the Hundred Years War, literally drained the population of Paris and of the country in general. In 1356, King John the Good was captured in battle by the English. A fearful Paris, now home to between 100,000 and 150,000 citizens, turned to Etienne Marcel, a wealthy merchant and experienced leader. He immediately organized the Parisian militia, established a supply network, and fortified the city, which had outgrown the wall built by Philip Augustus more than two centuries earlier.

Etienne Marcel administered the city with intelligence and authority. He then tried to leverage his power into the establishment of a permanent council in which the bourgeoisie would share decision-making in France with the ecclesiastics and the nobility. The idea of dividing their prerogatives further was distasteful to the royal family, and they used every means at their disposal—delaying tactics, deceit, bribery, and murder—to maintain absolute power. Etienne Marcel and his supporters were slain in 1358, and their properties were confiscated by the royal family. At the same time, in the countryside, a group known as the Jacques led a peasant insurrection against the nobility. It, too, ended with much blood being spent. These events—particularly those surrounding Etienne Marcel—are sometimes likened to those of the French Revolution. Although Marcel did benefit from the support of the Parisians, he represented an urban elite and, at no time, envisaged the overthrow of the monarchy. Not until 1789 would the bourgeoisie again be in a position of power.

URBAN DEVELOPMENT

During the second half of the 14th century, Charles V (r. 1364–1380) transformed the Louvre donjon into a Gothic-style manor. Since it stood at the western entrance to Paris, it remained heavily fortified. It was also during his reign that the Bastille was constructed, not as a prison but as a fort guarding the city on the east. From this gate, the high road, Rue Saint-Antoine, led into town. The wall protecting the right bank, begun by Etienne Marcel, was extended and strengthened. Chains were strung across the Seine as added protection against invaders. Charles V abandoned the Conciergerie on the Ile de la Cité: fearful of a turbulent population and anxious to distance himself from certain unpleasant memories for, as pretender to the throne at the time of his father's capture by the English and Etienne Marcel's takeover of the city, he had been intimately involved in the stormy events of that era.

On the right bank, in the area called the Marais (Marshes), which had been drained in the 13th century, he created the Hôtel Saint-Paul: a vast and luxurious palace of gardens, vineyards, royal suites, and reception halls, complemented by a menagerie with lions and an aviary. All have since been dismantled or destroyed, but the urban elite of the time followed him to the right bank, building "country" estates among the vineyards and fields. To some extent, these palatial residences counterbalanced the churches, monasteries, and colleges that dominated the left bank. In fact, the Hôtel Saint-Paul might be seen as the counter-weight to Notre-Dame, a configuration indicative of the under-lying power struggle between the secular and the religious.

At the end of the Middle Ages, the population of this very Gothic capital was no longer solely dependent on royal initiative.

The feudal city belonging to the royal domain, inhabited by crafts- and tradespersons dealing in farm produce, had been overtaken by urbanization. Hundreds of new skills and professions had appeared—the first shopkeepers, for example, as opposed to vendors. Wealth was amassed by a merchant class on whom the Capetian kings would lean for financial support. The monarchy, in turn, realized that its survival depended upon holding the reins of power ever tighter.

The Bastille. Begun in 1370, the Bastille was the largest of six forts built by Charles V to defend Paris. By the time of the French Revolution, it had become a prison.

Hôtel Saint-Paul, as it appeared in the 14th century. Charles V bought a number of noble houses on the right bank, near the Bastille, which he turned into a luxurious, walled compound. Nothing remains of the palace or two churches he built except the names they gave streets and métro stations.

Infighting

Charles VI (r. 1380–1422) was crowned King of France at the age of twelve. However, he exercised his charge effectively for only a few of the forty-two years of his reign. During his minority, his uncles held the reins of power, and clashes between the Parisians and the monarchy were frequent and violent.

Taxes were the issue of dispute. The life style of the royal house could no longer be supported by property revenues alone. Since the bourgeoisie rejected direct taxation, the royal house, resorted to indirect or sales taxes. On February 28, 1382, town criers at the main intersections of the city informed the public that merchandise taxes would be introduced the following day. The arrival of tax collectors at the central market signaled the start of an insurrectional movement that was to pit the common people and the bourgeoisie against the monarchy. The repression that followed was brutal, and whatever privileges the bourgeoisie had retained following Etienne Marcel's interregnum were further restricted.

Following his majority, Charles VI dismissed his uncles. He wed the beautiful Isabel of Bavaria and, together, they developed an immoderate taste for luxury and pleasure. The consequences were disastrous. Charles lost his mind and, from 1392 until his death thirty years later, he was incapable of exercising power effectively. The vacuum was filled by uncles, cousins, and brothers. As various factions competed for power, clans formed and rivalries became heated, with sometimes deadly results.

In 1407 the Duke of Orleans, the king's brother, was murdered on orders from John of Burgundy, Charles' uncle. The ensuing conflict between partisans of the Duke of Orleans (known as the Armagnacs) and those of John of Burgundy (Bourguignons or Burgundians) forced Parisians to take sides.

The Old Louvre. In the early 14th century, the Louvre was a very medieval castle, as can be seen above.

An alliance was eventually formed between John, known as the Fearless, the University, and the Butcher's Guild of Paris for the purpose of halting subsidies for the war (Hundred Years War) against England, as well as for the reform of the city administration. Under the leadership of Simon Caboche, the butchers attacked the Hôtel Saint-Paul, City Hall, and the Bastille. Men loyal to the Armagnacs were arrested and executed. Cabochian violence finally provoked the departure of numerous notables, while others worked for reconciliation between the warring royal factions.

The tide eventually turned against the rebellion. Strengthened by support from the future Charles VII and the armies of Louis of Bavaria and the Duke of Brittany, the Armagnacs marched onto the capital. Confusion was such that John and the Bourgundians withdrew from the city. The Armagnacs and their allies occupied Paris, ransacking and mutilating their opponents.

The vast reforms sought by the Cabochians, included in a vanguard document aimed at simplifying the administration, strengthening the judicial system, and cleaning up the finances of the city, were never enacted. For seven years, turmoil and civil war continued between factions of the royal family. The effects on Paris were disastrous: supply lines were cut and unemployment was extensive. Those who could took flight, among them the pretender to the throne, the future Charles VII.

Place de Grève. Public executions by hanging were frequent occurrences in the Middle Ages. The Place de Grève, or Place du Châtelet as it is now called, was often the scene of such spectacles, heavily attended by Parisians of the time.

ENGLISH RULE

For a good part of the 14th century, the history of Paris, as of France, was played out against the background of an off-and-on war with England and all that armed conflict necessarily implied in the way of recruitment, finance, ruin, and deprivation. However, the very sovereigns who fought for control of the western part of the European continent had inter-married for centuries. The nationalism that would later affect relations between England and France was of little note at the time. The general sentiment was that these events were a sort of "family affair."

Parallel to the civil war in France, Henry V of England had been preparing an attack on Paris. Despite being outnumbered three to one, the English army decimated the French in Normandy and took the Duke of Orleans prisoner. Henry V subsequently took Paris with scarcely a fight and, according to the terms of a treaty signed with Charles VI in 1420, he became regent of France and heir to the crown upon the mad king's death. Charles VI's son—the future Charles VII—was thereby eliminated from the line of succession. In addition, Henry V received the hand of Charles VI's daughter in marriage. Two years later, both kings were dead. Henry VI was crowned king of France at the age of one. His uncle, the Duke of Bedford, ruled in his stead until his own death in 1435.

Charles VII, however, had never abdicated his right to the throne. The Armagnacs continued to fight the Burgundians and the English on his behalf. It was at this point in history that Joan of Arc appeared on the scene. How much of her story is reality and how much legend remains difficult to ascertain. She certainly believed in her mission, which was to raise the siege of the city of Orleans and to see Charles VII crowned king at Rheims, in the

Joan of Arc (1412–1431). The above statue was the work of the 19ᵗʰ-century sculptor Henri Chapu.

cathedral that had witnessed the coronation of French kings until England's Henry V. The true miracle of Joan's adventure was her ability to convince an apathetic Charles VII and his counselors to provide her with a small troop, which was just enough to tip the balance of power. Within a matter of days, the English were gone from Orleans. Two and one-half months later, on July 17, 1429, the coronation took place at Rheims. Joan of Arc was later arrested, tried, and burned at the stake. Charles VII made not the slightest effort to save her.

Contrary to legend, however, these events were not the turning point of the war. The English and the Burgundians did not suddenly lose heart and abandon the fight. The war for Paris and the region dragged on for another six years. Only with the defection of the Duke of Burgundy to the king's side in 1435 was Charles finally able to recover Paris. The war continued elsewhere until 1453, when the French finally drove the English out of the provinces that surrounded Bordeaux, which they had held for three centuries.

Painting of the burning of Jeanne d'Arc at Rouen, which hangs in the Pantheon. Following a trial during which she defended herself with simplicity and courage, she was burned at the stake in 1431.

War's Consequences

Paris had suffered immensely. Its economy had ground to a halt, and food was scarce. The people were ill from malnutrition, and plagued by poverty, crime, and epidemics. In 1438, 50,000 people died from pestilential disease. It was forbidden to sound the church bells, so numerous were the funerals. Wolves entered Paris searching for flesh. Nonetheless, religion maintained its hold. Young women still volunteered to be immured in tombs in the Innocents Cemetery, to await death while praying for the souls of the departed.

Even pleasure had its macabre side. Parisians delighted in burlesque events that combined Christian events with pagan debauchery. On the occasion of a pious procession, for example, nothing appeared amiss in pitting a pig against a few blind men armed with sticks. The people flocked to tournaments, farcical theater, and executions.

Though still the capital, Paris became a city without a royal function. Both Charles VII (r. 1422–1461) and his son Louis XI (r. 1461–1483) planted the monarchal seat in the Loire Valley. The population of Paris recovered but economic activity faltered as the nobility, and thus the merchants who catered to them, deserted the city. Lawyers and functionaries took over.

Warfare and the king had broken the back of the merchant class. The influence of the Church had waned. The fortune of the feudal lords and the nobility was much diminished, and the reins of power were ever more tightly held by the Crown.

CHAPTER 5

ENTERING A NEW AGE

THE RENAISSANCE

The 15th century witnessed a Paris still reveling in its role of the medieval city par excellence. Its churches, its palaces and manors, and its private housing remained Gothic, marked by crenellated walls, spiral staircases, corner turrets, rib vaults, and gargoyles. The various trades—clothiers, grocers, furriers, jewelers, etc.—maintained their corporative structures.

Louis XI did order the leveling of the mountains of garbage, muck, and detritus that dotted the city and diffused horrific odors and maladies for noble and plebeian alike. Despite this effort and the creation of new boulevards, the overall aspect of the city was well entrenched.

Change, however, was in the offing. In 1470 the first print shop opened on the left bank. Books could be produced cheaply and relatively quickly. Fearful of the written word, the Crown instituted strict censorship. Nonetheless there was an outpouring of printed matter: bibles, almanacs, novels, and even flyers that announced the events of the day. Poets' claimed their "corners"; "thinkers" made themselves heard. The intellectual was being recognized as such and would gradually play a more significant role than either the artisan or the merchant.

Hôtel de Sens. This former archbishop's residence, which now houses the Forney Library of the Arts, is one of the rare 15th-century buildings in Paris to have survived. With its turrets, towers, gables, and arches, it is typical of the residence of a wealthy Parisian family in medieval Paris.

The new century coincided with the new era: the Renaissance. From Italy came a strong wind of change, brought to France in the wake of its rulers' lengthy and unsuccessful military campaigns. Charles VIII (r. 1483–1498) had launched a disastrous military campaign there in 1495. His army had pillaged and brought back trophies but had taken no territory. Louis XII (r. 1498–1515) felt the lure of Italy as well and became embroiled in a protracted military adventure that ended in frustration and withdrawal. King Francis I (r. 1515–1547) also had his Italian sprees—four wars in all, all disastrous and all costly.

The French did, however, gain in wonderment: they experienced the Italian Renaissance, saw art and science from a new perspective, and acquired an understanding of the organization and role of a capital. They were cowed by the physical and intellectual wealth of the world surrounding the Mediterranean and, upon their return home, recognized Paris for the medieval city that it was. Well into the 16th century the Italian experience would be drawn upon for Paris' transformation. French artists would travel to Italy to study the masters. Italian artists, sculptors, ceramicists such as della Robbia, theater groups, engineers, architects, bankers, politicians, and prelates thronged to France. (It was at this time that Francis I purchased the *Mona Lisa* from Leonardo da Vinci.)

Their imprint on French society was indelible; in addition to all else, they injected a humanistic element. Style and fashion changed, and morals were affected. The lottery was introduced, a stock exchange created, and several banks opened. Even writing was modernized, passing from the stiff, Gothic script to Roman and italic characters. The horizontal replaced the Gothic vertical. Gone was the vaulted arch. Symmetry was the order of the day. Buildings would be of equal height and appearance, and streets would be wider and straighter, for the horse-drawn coach had arrived from Italy! Sanitation, too, required new measures: the entrances to houses were to be paved and washed regularly; drainage systems were consolidated and extended; and garbage collectors made their appearance as a profession.

The city was recalling its Roman past. Its heroes returned from war not to the sounds and cries of a Christian bazaar, but to the decorum of the antique gates of an Italian city.

Since the departure of the English at the end of the Hundred Years War (mid-1400s), French monarchs had felt sufficiently strong to govern from any point in their territory. After his defeat and imprisonment in Italy, however, Francis I needed to establish a firm base in the north. He also needed money to defend his northern frontier and to counter the Austrians to the east. In 1528 he made the following declaration to his people: "Very dear and beloved, our intention is, from now on, to make the greatest part of our residence and stay in our good city of Paris and its surroundings more than in any other place of the realm." This appeal marks the beginning of the Ancien Régime (Old or Former Regime), which would endure until 1789. In the meantime, Parisians would stand behind their king.

Francis I set about extending and enhancing the Louvre. The original donjon was razed to allow more light to enter the quadrangle; windows were enlarged; and an extended, new palace was designed in Renaissance style by Pierre Lescot. The king also ordered the construction of a new city hall.

The king had verve, charm, and a propensity for the extravagant and the opulent. Although he settled officially in Paris, he still spent considerable time in the Loire Valley moving from one castle to the next. The nobility, short of funds, could no longer maintain their past life style of splendor; they clung to the king and lived off him. Thus came into being the court, which would survive as long as the monarchy.

The Conciergerie, as it was in the middle of the 16th century, at about the time Francis I commissioned architect Pierre Lescot to begin plans for a new Renaissance palace to replace the Louvre donjon and its appendages.

THE REFORMATION

The Protestantism of Luther and Calvin arrived in Paris in the 16th century on the heels of the printing press and the humanism of the Renaissance. The first martyr—or first heretic, as Jean Vallière's persecutors were to call him—claimed by the new ideas was burned at the stake in Paris in 1523 for having impugned the immaculate conception, declaring that Jesus was the son of Joseph and Mary. Despite the violence of the Church's reaction, the new faith continued to attract intellectuals, artists, editors, teachers, and university students, as well as numerous members of the aristocracy, royal family, and the affluent elite. The working class and the unemployed, inhabitants of the right bank in the main, remained loyal to their Catholic roots. The reformers (or Huguenots, as they were derisively called) were tracked at first by the Sorbonne and parliament and later by the monarchy. Nonetheless, in 1555 in Paris, the Calvinists founded the reformed church.

While Francis I had sought to limit fanaticism, under his son and successor, Henry II (r. 1547–1559), persecution of so-called heretics was ruthless. Despite the concerted efforts, 2,150 reformed churches existed in France by 1561. In an amazing show of strength, 15,000 Parisians assembled that year in the suburbs of Paris for a Calvinist sermon. Then, on May 1, 1562, 200 Protestants were massacred by soldiers of the Duke de Guise on a country estate in the Champagne region, east of Paris. The first war of religion had begun; there would be eight in all, the last in 1595.

One of the most odious events of this long, drawn-out struggle occurred in 1572, during the celebrations surrounding the marriage of Henry, the King of Navarre, and the sister of King

Charles IX of France, Marguerite de Valois. This union between the Protestant king and the Catholic princess was seen as a foundation upon which peace between the warring factions might rest. However, the arrival in Paris of numerous Protestant personalities whet the appetite of extremist elements among the "Papists"—the term used by the reformers to identify the Catholic population. With the agreement of the queen mother, Catherine de Médicis, and Charles IX, the city gates were closed the night before Saint Bartholemew's Day. Early the following morning, the slaughter of Parisian and foreign Protestants began. Members of parliament, university professors, students, doctors, and lawyers were slain in their beds and in the streets. Estimates of the number killed range from two to ten thousand. Thus began the fourth war of religion.

The most powerful monarchy in Europe at the time was that of Philip II of Spain. Buttressed by the wealth of the New World, Spain dominated Italy and the Low Countries. The fervent nature of its Catholicism made it the ideal ally for the battle of the Counter-Reformation. On several occasions Philip II's contingents assisted the Parisians in holding the Protestant armies at bay. The King of Spain even entertained the idea of procuring the crown of France for his daughter Isabella.

Paris, like France, was subjected to over thirty years of extremism, terrorism, deceit, and treachery, not to mention ignorance, intolerance, shame, for which the city paid a heavy price. In addition to the war's dead, 30,000 more people died as a result of a blockade put in place by the Protestant nobleman, Henry of Navarre. Expiring from his wounds on the battlefield at Saint-Cloud, on the outskirts of Paris, Henry III (r. 1574–1589) designated Henry of Navarre as his successor to the throne of France. Negotiations were entered into with the Church, and the king-

St. Germain l'Auxerrois. At two in the morning on St. Bartholomew's Feast Day 1572, the bell at St. Germain l'Auxerrois rang out as a signal for the massacre of Protestants to begin. The bloodbath lasted several days.

designate abjured his Protestant religion. He ordered the immediate departure of the Spanish army: "Leave and never return."

One of the first acts of Henry of Navarre, now King Henry IV (r. 1589–1610), was to promulgate the Edict of Nantes, which was meant to guarantee freedom of conscience and full equality before the law to all Protestants. The edict also provided for places of refuge within armed Protestant garrisons financed by the State, but it was never fully applied. It would take the French Revolution, two centuries hence, for the Reformed Church to gain effective freedom of worship and expression.

Paris was weary of war and, when Henry IV lifted the siege around the city, he was welcomed by cries of "peace and bread." However, neither the fanatics of the Catholic cause nor the Church hierarchy in Rome were ready to disarm. The king foiled seventeen assassination attempts over the years of his reign. He was eventually stabbed to death in Rue Ferronnerie on May 14, 1610. His assassin, François Ravaillac, was quartered in front of a massive crowd, which, unbridled, tore him from limb to limb before the executioner was able to set fire to the cadaver.

Statue of Henry IV, which stands on the Pont Neuf. Known to be lean, dry-humored and alert, Henry had been raised the hard way, "barefoot and hatless" alongside the village children of his native Béarn, in south-western France.

Urban Planning

Henry IV was the first of a new line of kings, the Bourbons. His reign was a fruitful one. The first modern attempts at city planning were introduced and overseen by the king himself. He elaborated the Grand Design, a project meant to encompass both the Louvre Palace and the Tuileries Palace, which was under construction in what are now the Tuileries Gardens. The two castles were to be joined by long galleries and to be surrounded by gardens and pavilions. The long gallery on the Seine was begun.

Another major project completed under Henry IV, in 1605, was the construction of the Pont Neuf from the left bank, through the Ile de la Cité, to the right bank. It was bordered by Paris' very first sidewalks and decorated with its first public statue: an equestrian, whose rider, Henry IV, would be placed upon it during the reign of his son. It was the first bridge in Paris constructed without dwellings on either side, a fashion that would soon be imitated throughout Europe. Parisians adored their new bridge. They danced and promenaded upon it, watched puppet shows and purchased flowers for their belles. For those who protested that the bridge led nowhere, Henry IV had the Rue Dauphine cut and ordered that houses be aligned and of similar facade. When a religious order refused to sell a lot it owned there, the king demanded that the wall around it be gone within twenty-four hours or he would fell it himself with cannon fire!

In 1607 he had the Place Dauphine designed, Italian in style and triangular in form. Then the Place Royale, today's Place des Vosges, came off the drawing boards: a perfect square surrounded by like buildings, with covered, arched galleries on all four sides. Hitherto, the squares of Paris had not been conceived, but had come about by chance. While subjected to numerous

Pont Neuf. This first "modern" bridge of Paris was commissioned by Henry IV and completed in 1605.

Place des Vosges. Over the years, the square became home to numerous personalities, among them Madame de Sévigné, Jacques-Bénigne Bossuet, Victor Hugo, Alphonse Daudet, and Théophile Gautier. Originally called Place Royale, it was finally baptized Place des Vosges in honor of the first region of France to pay its taxes following the Revolution. Victor Hugo's house, shown in the photo, is now a museum.

regulations and taxes, houses and buildings had previously been set down in haphazard fashion.

Henry IV's son and successor, Louis XIII (r. 1610–1643), was also a builder. He completed the buildings around the *cour carrée*, or quadrangle of the Louvre, and ordered the construction of five new bridges across the Seine. It became fashionable to live in the Marais district of the right bank, in the vicinity of the Place Royale. New mansions blossomed in this section—among them, Hôtel Carnavalet (now the Museum of the City of Paris), Hôtel Lamoignon, and Hôtel de Sully (also a museum).

This was the age of the Counter-Reformation. Anxious to obliterate the memory of his father's Protestant background, Louis XIII encouraged Catholic institutions. During his reign, Paris was literally encircled by new churches, convents, and other religious buildings. On the left bank, doctor friends of Louis XIII created a garden of medicinal herbs, rose bushes, and vines on the king's behalf; it is now called the Plant Garden (Jardin des Plantes). Nearby, the Collège de France was housed in new quarters. Louis XIII's mother, Marie de Médicis, ordered the construction of the Luxembourg Palace and gardens, which were modeled after the Pitti Palace and Boboli Gardens of her native Florence. The Roman aqueduct, built some thirteen centuries earlier, was resuscitated to keep her gardens moist.

Curiously enough, builders as they were, both Henry IV and Louis XIII promulgated ordinances prohibiting construction throughout the city. To their minds, Paris was sufficiently populated and needed air and open space. But no text could restrain the builders, and Paris continued to grow inside and outside its walls.

No records of population statistics exist for the period preceding the French Revolution. However, from the study of tax rolls and from estimates of population density, the figure of

400,000 inhabitants has been advanced as a reasonable one for the time. They would have dwelled in some 17,000 houses along the city's 600 streets. Those involved in trade and commerce counted for the largest sector of the population. Sixty thousand were craftspeople of some kind, including carpenters, cabinet-makers, weavers, spinners, drapers, dyers, shoemakers, furriers, dressmakers and tailors, perfumers, gunsmiths, and metal-workers. It was time for Paris to produce its own luxury goods and art objects, and to enter into competition with articles imported from abroad. Hence, in the new long gallery of the Louvre, which bordered the Seine, Henry IV invited watchmakers, goldsmiths, painters, and sculptors to install their studios. Louis XIII added the mint and the royal printing house to that wing of the palace.

WINDS OF CHANGE

In 1624, Louis XIII designated Cardinal de Richelieu head of government. For eighteen years, Richelieu ruled with an iron hand. Protestants lost their safeguards. Executions were the rule for noblemen who defied his authority, and he was no less harsh with the common people. He amassed a considerable fortune along the way, even creating a new neighborhood to the west of the Louvre. In the center of the land he built his own residence, the Palais-Cardinal, now the Palais-Royal. Upon his death in 1642, he was replaced by his right hand man, Giulio Mazarini, a Sicilian who was Jesuit-educated in Spain and held the title of cardinal (procured for him by Richelieu). The French called him Mazarin. When Louis XIII met an early death in 1643, Mazarin took over both the queen-regent and the country.

Richelieu's military campaigns during the Thirty Years War (1618–1648) had required heavy financing, which engendered increased taxation. The people of Paris—the working people and the elite alike—held no love for Richelieu and little for the monarch he served. His successor, Mazarin, whose penchant for luxury did not escape notice and who amassed an even greater fortune than Richelieu—a scandalous fortune, historians stress—laid down new and additional taxes. Then, in 1648, Mazarin informed the members of the three existing royal courts that the state would not pay their salaries for the next four years. Although parliament was not concerned directly by this measure, it displayed immediate solidarity by convening a meeting of the four bodies, the express purpose of which was "to reform State abuses." A document, called the Union Act, was elaborated in which parliament demanded to be privy to the affairs of the nation and claimed the right to act upon such. The act was revolutionary. For the first time, a separation of

The entrance to the Palais-Cardinal (now Palais-Royal), built between 1620 and 1630 by Cardinal Richelieu as his personal residence.

powers was being prescribed. The king was the nation, and the realm had always been inseparable from his person. Neither the sovereign's domain, nor his power, were shareable. The Union Act could, in principle, lead to monarchy's demise.

It should be noted that parliament, created in the middle of the 13th century, was in no way a representative assembly in the modern sense. It functioned only as a court of law. Composed of magistrates drawn from a wealthy and powerful elite, it rendered justice in the name of the king. Its decisions could, however, be overturned by the King's Council.

Parisians rallied behind parliament, and Mazarin, fearful of a popular uprising, acceded to most of the demands formulated in the Union Act. He then bided his time and, on the occasion of a victory celebration at Notre-Dame Cathedral (August 26, 1648), had a number of parliament members arrested. Several tumultuous days of barricades and negotiations followed, after which Mazarin, the queen-regent, and young Louis XIV secretly fled the city.

Parliament reacted by proclaiming Mazarin a "public enemy," setting up its own government and calling upon the people to take up arms. Mazarin countered the city's new battalions with the royal army, which blockaded Paris and ransacked the country homes of the bourgeois elite. Parliament was forced to negotiate and, on March 11, 1649, signed a treaty by which it renounced any further independent action "on any pretext whatsoever."

This period in French history, from 1648 until 1653, is known as *La Fronde*, which literally means "the sling," but which could also be translated as "the winds of change." It was a particularly confused period during which loyalties changed rapidly. The goal of parliament had been to create a regime based on the rule of law rather than on the king's will. When their struggle received the benediction of certain noblemen, its character changed into a struggle of feudal masters against the monarchy.

The plots, sub-plots, and intrigues elaborated during this period were many. The Bishop of Paris, disgruntled by the fact that his long-awaited nomination as cardinal had not been honored, turned his back on Mazarin and supported parliament. Several noble ladies injected a note of romanticism in the struggle and, despite the apparent frivolity of their efforts, managed to influence some members of the nobility to attack Mazarin in various parts of France. No better example of a turncoat exists than that of Louis de Condé, head of the royal army that had saved Mazarin from a rebellious Paris, who then turned against Mazarin and was later arrested by him.

Finally, when the coalition of interests against him proved too powerful, Mazarin withdrew to Cologne, Germany. He was a masterful tactician, however, and released Condé from prison upon leaving France. The latter immediately demanded that he be accepted as the head of the insurrection, and thus sole ruler of Paris. The parliamentary magistrates and the nobility soon found themselves at loggerheads, however, whereas the bishop finally received his award and, as Cardinal de Retz, rejoined the side of the queen-regent and Mazarin.

By 1652 Parisians were starving; they were sick of war and strife. Partisans and adversaries of the winds of change rioted. Condé, whose army had been engaged in a campaign against the monarchy throughout France, returned to Paris ready to exercise his authority as leader of *La Fronde*. However, the various other players in this drama were by then in agreement to accept the authority of young king Louis XIV (r. 1643–1715) on condition that Mazarin be revoked. Finally, in October of that year, Condé quit the capital and placed himself and his men under the protection of the Spanish army in central France. Louis XIV entered Paris and from the Louvre issued a pronouncement that parliament was henceforth never to interfere in affairs of the state nor in those concerning the royal finances. In February 1653, Mazarin returned in triumph to Paris. The wheel had gone full circle: revolution was not to be.

CHAPTER 6

POWER AND MONARCHY

LOUIS XIV

Upon reaching his majority in 1654, Louis XIV became the reigning king of France at the age of sixteen. However, until Mazarin's death in 1661, he did not effectively exercise leadership. By then the nobility had been rendered subservient, parliament impotent, and France was the dominant power in Europe. In fact, Paris seemed so secure that Louis XIV ordered the city's ramparts dismantled and the resulting gaps to be filled with trees. (They would become the Grands Boulevards.) Even though Paris was, for the time being, an "open city," the ordinances restricting construction remained in place.

In the beginning of his reign, Parisians had welcomed Louis XIV with enthusiasm. However, their euphoria waned quickly and then plummeted during the Fouquet Affair of 1661. Superintendent of Finance during Mazarin's reign, Fouquet was accused of large-scale financial irregularities. The fervor with which Jean-Baptiste Colbert, the Superintendent of Finance, had the case prosecuted surrounded Fouquet with the aura of a martyr. Even parliament felt disinclined, on the basis of what it considered insubstantial evidence, to deal a heavy sentence. The court ultimately sentenced

Fouquet to banishment, but its verdict was overruled by the monarch and changed to life imprisonment. Parisians expressed their disappointment with the harsh judgment. To quote Madame de Sévigné, "our master's severe aspect inspires more fear than hope."

In March 1667 the position of Police Lieutenant was created for Nicolas de La Reynie. As head of the Parisian administration he was to be responsible for public order, justice, health, sanitation, and the economy in general. Chief among his duties, however, was that of preventing any expression of disapproval! The authors and propagators of critical flyers or news sheets were flogged, banished, or, in extreme cases, employed as galley slaves.

La Fronde, whatever its shortcomings, had far-reaching consequences for the future of Paris and of France. Louis XIV and his successors were to harbor deep feelings of mistrust towards the city and its people. Paris became a scourge, a disgrace, and in many ways the enemy. The king's mindset was such that from the time he installed himself and his court at Versailles in 1671, to the time of his death forty-four years later, he visited Paris but twenty-four times and never for more than a few hours. In the last fifteen years of his life, he laid eyes on the capital city of France exactly four times.

Versailles was the true center of Louis XIV's realm. Though only four leagues distant as the crow flies, the two towns were two to three hours apart by coach. Versailles began as Louis XIII's modest hunting lodge, built of rose-colored brick and stone. In 1660, one year after his marriage to Maria Teresa, daughter of Philip IV of Spain, Louis XIV took the momentous decision to transform the lodge into the palace of palaces. He commissioned the finest artists of the time: the architect Louis LeVau, the landscape architect Le Nôtre, and the painter-decorator Charles Le

Marriage of Madame de Maintenon and Louis XIV. After many years of attending to the education of Louis XIV's illegitimate children, Françoise Scarron arrived at Court with her charges. She later wed the king as Madame de Maintenon. Her influence, rigid and pious, reinforced the generally melancholic atmosphere at Versailles in the latter years of Louis XIV's regency.

Brun. Jules Hardouin-Mansart took over as architect upon LeVau's death in 1670. Initiated when Louis XIV was twenty-three years old, construction would continue for fifty years. Thirty-seven thousand acres of marshland were drained. The Bièvre River was diverted to feed the 1,400 fountains. A vast, complicated hydraulic system was invented to drain off water from the Seine. One hundred and fifty thousand plants were bedded, and 100 statues placed in the gardens alone. Thirty-five thousand workers were still on the job when the king and his court took up residence in 1671.

The court numbered 20,000 at the time. This figure included 9,000 soldiers billeted in the town, and 5,000 servants in an annex. One thousand noble men and women and their 4,000 servants were housed at the palace. Louis XIV oversaw the entire establishment personally. During Mazarin's lifetime, he had been reserved and had rarely intervened in affairs of state. However, upon the chief minister's death in 1661, when asked to whom his staff should report in the future, Louis XIV replied unhesitatingly: "To me." And so it was in matters large and small.

The sums lavished on Versailles were colossal. Almost ten times more was spent there than on Paris during Louis XIV's entire reign, despite the fact that Superintendent Colbert had great visions for the city which he imagined as the "new" Rome. Louis once announced to the Petite Académie, a type of ministry of culture: "Gentlemen, you can appreciate the esteem in which I hold you by the fact that I have entrusted to you the thing I hold dearest in the world: my glory." This statement was not so surprising—he had, in 1662, chosen for himself the motto of *le roi soleil* (The Sun King).

So it was that two societies came about. The seat of power and intrigue developed around the king at Versailles. The ministries moved from Paris. Leading families and courtesans emigrated. Even music was transported to Versailles, for to achieve prominence as a musician required the court's stamp of approval and the king's largess. Jean-Baptiste Lully, creator of the French opera, arrived from Florence, Henri Du Mont from Belgium, and the prominent French musicians Richard Delalande and François Couperin from Paris.

The noted playwrights Nicolas Boileau and Jean Racine were engaged by Louis XIV as historiographers and accompanied him on military campaigns. According to Boileau, the monarch's crossing of the Rhine on June 12, 1672, as he marched on Holland, was an epic event—one later disavowed by Voltaire: "May I ask you pardon for having said that there were forty or fifty feet to swim across the Rhine. There were only twelve."

When Louis XIV awoke in the morning or bedded down at night, and as he took his meals, his court and public looked on. His life was a show, and he incessantly turned to the left and to the right to observe those in attendance. Absences were marked, and Louis' "It's someone I never see" was tantamount to banishment. Reactions to the Versailles routine varied from that of the Duchess of Soubise—"How could one live anywhere else but at court?"—to that of Madame Sévigné, who refused to become "a court monkey."

The *beau monde* remaining in Paris moved to the Faubourg Saint-Germain on the left bank of the Seine. The *nouveaux riches* continued to settle in the Marais or Montmartre, while the rest of the population crammed into the center of the city. For apprentices and workers, life was not easy. Their mainstay, bread, represented sixty percent of their food budget. As the price of meat was prohibitive, the rest of their diet consisted of soup and perhaps, on Fridays, fish.

Paris was also home to hordes of vagrants and beggars, generally transplants from poorer rural areas. In the middle of the 17th century, they represented approximately one-tenth of the city's population. At any one time 10,000 people were incarcerated at the Hôpital-général, a prison for vagrants picked off the streets by the police. The city organized public works projects and the Church ran charities that were often more effective than the city's bureaucratic endeavors. Vagabonds were also put aboard ship and transported to France's New World colonies, often as indentured servants.

In 1667, oil lamps were introduced in certain streets. However, the center of the city remained dangerous. The Court of Miracles, an area frequented by thieves and cut-throats, was ordered destroyed; but nothing—certainly not the city's small, poorly organized police force—could obliterate the underworld as such.

There were other unpleasant aspects to city life at the time, namely the stench and disease. The rivers surrounding and within Paris were the public sewers and dumps of city dwellers, slaughter houses, tanners, and pig farmers. Cemeteries bulged with mass graves in which decomposed bodies were barely hidden from sight.

La Reynie, the city's Police Lieutenant, attempted to improve sanitation. He hired more garbage collectors and street sweepers, while designating specific areas at the city limits as dumps. He transferred the skeletons of the Innocents Cemetery to the Catacombs' underground quarries. But his efforts made little impression. Walking still meant slithering in mud and filth, as most streets were unpaved and Parisians continued to throw refuse, including the contents of their chamber pots, out the window. Water shortages remained a chronic problem. Houses, even manors and chateaux, lacked the most elementary sanitation—better it was to reek of perfume than to bathe. As for public health, the wealthy could avail themselves of doctors' services. Their efficacy was questionable, but they were nonetheless preferable to the ghastly hospitals of the time. In short, there was a seamy side to the glorious reign of the Sun King.

For him, divine right was not a vain term. Even his birth embodied something of the miraculous. Louis XIII and Anne of Austria (Spanish by birth) had shared little intimacy during their marriage, and the accident of her pregnancy could well be considered providential.

Louis XIV was of mediocre intelligence. However, he surrounded himself with the better minds of the time and he heeded their advice. Meetings of the Royal Council were not exercises in rubberstamping. But when decisions were finally taken—slowly was the rule—they were his own.

Whatever the weight of Versailles, Paris was the capital of France and could not be forsaken. On the contrary, Louis XIV was adamant that his imprint on Paris be recognized by posterity. The symbols and constructions of his reign were secular, inspired not by Gothic ecclesiasticism but by classic Rome. Expansion to the west of the city, towards Versailles, became paramount.

Le Nôtre, the landscape architect and master of perspective, extended the Tuileries to the west, felling trees and ripping up kitchen gardens to create an extended, broad avenue that apparently led nowhere. Originally baptized Avenue des Tuileries, it soon took on the flattering name of Avenue des Champs-Elysées, though these Elysian Fields long remained a muddy road frequented by Parisian low life. Le Nôtre also designed the Rond-Point. To the east of the city, a new boulevard entrance to Paris had been laid out for the arrival of the monarch and his bride in 1660; it ran from the Bastille to the Place du Trône, through the woods to the Château de Vincennes. All of these projects supplanted the north-south orientation of Paris that had been in place since the time of the Roman occupation.

Whereas Henry IV had developed the triangle for the Place Dauphine and the square for the Place Royale, the circle and the octagon gained privilege under Louis XIV. The Place des Victoires designed by Hardouin-Mansart encircled a 35-feet tall statue of Louis XIV crowned by Immortality! The original plan for the Place Vendôme was for a square resembling a theater stage, with an opening on one side. The facades, not the buildings themselves, were constructed in 1686 and left empty. Few of the plots found buyers, however, and the facades were dismantled in 1699. Hardouin-Mansart then redesigned an octagonal square open at each end, with ionic columns gracing the new facades. In the center a statue of Louis XIV was erected, wearing Roman garb and a Renaissance wig. The plots around the square were high-priced and acquired almost exclusively by wealthy financiers.

The Louvre, abandoned for Versailles, was sorely in need of attention. Inhabited by artists and courtesans, stables, archives, and academies, as well as pigeons and rats, its grounds were occupied by huts, lean-tos, and shops. The eastern end of the palace, in which the royal apartments were located, had been intended as the main entrance leading into the *cour carrée*. Colbert invited Bernini, the famous Italian architect, to Paris. However, his project was rejected—unfortunately so according to many. Today's classic colonnade was designed by Claude Perrault. But rather than open the Louvre to the east, where an elegant avenue was to have led to City Hall, it actually enclosed it, creating a false front.

The gem of edifices constructed during Louis XIV's reign was undoubtedly the Invalides, a veterans home designed by Libéral

Bruant. Once military glory waned, regiments were dispersed and soldiers without domicile or pay swelled the ranks of the destitute. According to an ordinance signed in 1674, "nothing is more capable of discouraging those who would be willing to bear arms, to embrace this profession, than to see the nasty condition to which have been reduced most of those who, having joined and possessing nothing, have become aged or maimed, if we did not take care of their subsistence and maintenance as is our resolve to do. . . ." At its peak, 4,000 old soldiers were billeted at the Invalides. The men were organized into workshops and supplied the city with various objects and clothing of their making. Discipline was severe, however, and the community spirit gradually flagged.

The Wars

Louis XIV had a thirst for glory and prestige; moreover, he suffered no slight. France fought four wars during his time, covering some thirty of the fifty-four years of his reign. The first war, begun in 1667, was with Spain over a matter concerning Queen Maria Teresa's substantial unpaid dowry and her rights to territory in her own name. France's armies immediately took Flanders—Spanish Netherlands at the time—only to find themselves facing a triple alliance of England, Holland, and Sweden. The king made peace the following year, keeping territory that is today part of Belgium. Decidedly dissatisfied with the outcome, he attacked Holland in 1672. The Dutch defended themselves with genius by opening the dikes and flooding the country. What had started as a punitive expedition quickly turned into a full-blown European war, the Dutch War. After seven years of battle, France occupied sufficient territory in the east for Louis XIV to claim victory. In 1681 he incorporated the eastern territories into France, Strasbourg included.

Throughout Louis XIV's reign religious controversy continued to be intense. Jesuits vied with the very rigorous orthodox apostles of predestination, the Jansenists, while Rome fought to curtail the independence of the French clergy and its justice system. Protestants remained on their guard, though some among them had climbed to the upper reaches of the regime as army generals, admirals, and marshals. Bit by bit the Edict of Nantes, Henry IV's guarantee of religious freedom and safety to Protestants, was shredded. Conversion to Catholicism was required. Violence returned with a vengeance. In 1684 cavalry units sought out recalcitrant Calvinists, dismembering them in their homes. In 1685, Louis officially revoked the Edict of Nantes triggering the mass exodus of Protestants. Skilled craftspeople, merchants, and intellectuals left for Germany, Switzerland, England, Holland, South Africa, and the New World. Revolts against the monarchy broke out in the Languedoc, Cahors, and the Cévennes.

Throughout 17th-century Europe, the struggle between Protestantism and Catholicism remained very much alive. In 1688 a Protestant, William of Orange, replaced the Stuart royalty and became King of England. He succeeded in uniting much of the continent against Louis XIV under the banner of the Grand Alliance. War raged for over ten years, during which period French taxes were raised many times. Harvests were poor and speculators cornered the market, increasing the price of grain fivefold. In 1695, so desperate was the situation that three eminent Frenchmen wrote to the monarch: "Your people, Sire, whom you should love like your children . . . are dying of hunger . . . You have destroyed half the real forces within your State in order to make and defend vain conquests outside." The Treaty of Ryswick, signed in 1697, changed little with respect to the territorial limits of France. Louis XIV had failed, however, and his reputation and country were in ruins. But he would not be downed.

In 1701 Carlos II of Spain, who was childless, bequeathed his realm and its far-flung colonies to Philip of Anjou, the grandson of Louis XIV. This action enraged Austria and Bavaria, which could also hold claims to the Spanish empire through the female line. Treaty negotiations for the purpose of dividing the empire failed, whereupon Louis claimed it as his own. War ensued against another European Grand Alliance, composed of England and Austria. To raise money for the conflict, Louis sold off titles and charges, and borrowed from Parisian bankers. Even his gold table service was melted down for bullion.

In military terms, this final war of his reign, the War of the Spanish Succession (1701–1714), was not the disaster it might have been. Louis' grandson retained the Spanish throne, and the French realm remained intact, despite the loss of overseas possessions such as Arcadia, Hudson Bay, and Newfoundland. On the home front, however, things could not have been worse. Fiscal pressure was tremendous and poverty extreme, as French industry ground to a halt. The harsh winter of 1709 was particularly horrifying. The Seine froze over and wheat deliveries to Paris were blocked from January to April. In August, the royal house announced the beginning of excavation work to assist the poor. By four A.M. the following day, 6,000 unemployed people were on line for recruitment. Their pay was to be three pounds of bread and two sous per day, but the bread soon ran out. The workers rioted and soldiers attacked them, whereupon 15,000 men and women armed with sticks marched on the central market. Musketeers and other armed militia held them at bay and occupied the major intersections of Paris during the following months. What most disturbed the now senile king, however, were the posters placarded around the city, which attacked him, his conduct, and his government. When Louis XIV died on September 1, 1715, to quote the well-known French historian Saint-Simon: "the people, ruined, downtrodden, desperate, gave thanks to God."

Louis XV

Louis XIV's son and first grandchild having passed away before him, the crown fell to his great grandson, a child of five. Louis had foreseen that the regency would be exercised by his brother Philip, Duke of Orleans, for whom he felt no kindness. By will, he attempted to install one of his illegitimate sons as prince and regent. Philip would not be undone, however, and had parliament nullify Louis' testament, which act was to restore some of that institution's prerogatives. Philip returned the center of authority and the future monarch to Paris. He opened the prisons and freed the Jansenists and many commoners, at the same time that he cracked down on blackmailers, police prevaricators, and corrupt businesses. The people of Paris applauded.

The former regime had developed a strict, hypocritical moral posture, whereas the Regent opened wide the gates of pleasure and license in which, it seems, Philip partook to the full. The economy took an upward swing. The population was generally approving, despite a major scandal when the private bank of John Law, a daring, dashing, and scandal-bent Scottish financier and the General Controller of the Ministry of Finance, went bankrupt in 1719.

Another deplorable scandal during the Regency occurred in 1720 following an ordinance that called for the arrest of vagabonds, in particular "those who are young and in good health," to be transported to Louisiana. That spring 600 young men and women were embarked to the vast and largely unsettled French colony in America. A chronicler of the time wrote: "the boys walk in front, chained together two by two, the girls were in wagons. . . ." The people were aghast and rioted for several days, leading to a modification of the ordinance.

Upon Philip's death in 1723, the young king removed himself to Versailles. The motivation for this move, it seems, was the desire to control the nobility more closely by having the court under the king's roof again. Or perhaps it was simply to distance the sovereign from the gaze of the Parisian population.

As Louis XV (r. 1715–1774) was still too young to rule, the Duke of Bourbon took charge and became exceedingly unpopular. When Louis XV came of age, he relegated the affairs of city and state to his former tutor, the abbé Fleury. Only after his mentor's death in 1743, at the age of ninety, was the king to exercise power personally. The following year, as he left for eastern France to fight in the War of the Austrian Succession, he fell ill and Parisians prayed sincerely for his recovery. This popularity among the people was short-lived, however, as indifference was one of his main characteristics. He ignored his subjects and affairs of state were a bore to him with the exception of petty intrigue, for which he established his own secret police. Moreover Louis XV was licentious, much to the delight of the court. Madame de Pompadour, who managed to remain his favorite for some twenty years despite frequent competition, meddled freely in foreign affairs and cultural matters. Luckily for posterity, her artistic awareness was of quality.

Louis and his entourage, on the other hand, still saw world politics as a game of family succession. This view contributed to the four demeaning wars during his reign: the aftermath of the War of the Spanish Succession (1718–1720); the War of the Polish Succession (1733–1738); the War of the Austrian Succession (1740–1748); and the Seven Years War (1756–1763). Though the latter was also provoked by the Austrian Succession, the direct enemy was England. In this era of colonial expansion, England and France were vying for imperial supremacy in the New World and Asia. As a result of this last war, France was divested of its holdings in India and in Canada: "a few acres of snow," as Voltaire commented at the time.

Louis' attitude towards these occurrences is well summed up in his appearance on the battlefield at Fontenoy in 1745. With kingly courtesy and a flourish, he begged the English to fire the first shots of the battle. They assented, leaving 800 French soldiers dead.

The royal house intended that its military losses be kept under wraps, and "defeat" became a dirty word. Beginning in 1742, repression intensified and all printed matter was maintained under close surveillance. Considered too easily transportable and too silent by the Parisian police, the rolling press had been forbidden by royal decree since 1728. However, numerous handwritten flyers and gazettes, produced in Paris or brought in from German and Dutch cities, circulated under cover—all attacking the king and his government. In the city's cafés, notably those in the gardens of the Palais-Royal, the Luxembourg, and the Tuileries, the whispering campaigns were potent, as were the ditties of the *chansonniers* and the posters that appeared everywhere. Not surprisingly, informers were also numerous and sanctions heavy for those caught spreading an anti-government or anti-monarchal message.

Nonetheless opposition developed in every sector of public life. The parliamentary magistrates, critical of the administration of state finances, the constant imposition of new taxes, and the lack of a regular budget or any savings, insisted that their prerogatives be redefined. Grumbling was unabashed. Louis XV riposted by dissolving two of the five parliamentary courts, thereby provoking strikes of magistrates and lawyers. The defeat of the Seven Years War finally forced the king to accept a compromise solution;

Voltaire (1694–1778). Two mordant satires on the state of the nation appeared during the reign of the regent. Attributed to the young poet, Voltaire was imprisoned at the Bastille.

however, it did not include any jurisdiction over State finances. Louis' debts were gargantuan and, for the twentieth time during his reign, taxes were raised, this time three-fold! The tug of war between the Crown and parliament continued and, despite the fact that the population felt no particular fondness for the latter, they supported the quest to wrench some measure of decision-making power from the monarch.

It was not to be: in 1771, the magistrates were exiled from Paris and their offices confiscated. The judiciary was reorganized and new judges appointed. One commentator noted: "He included in his new Paris tribunal a mass of people disdained because of their bad reputations and the vulgarity of their former lifestyles, as well as their stultifying lack of talent."

State finances and parliamentary prerogative were not the only grounds for opposition to the monarchy. Religious strife also played its part. The principal influence both in Rome and the royal house was Jesuit, while the magistrates were solidly Jansenist, as were the majority of the common people, certain leading members of the bourgeoisie, and the local priests. This meant, in short, that the majority of the city was hostile to the perceived religious laxity of the Jesuits. Scenes of religious hysteria followed miracles revealed in a Parisian cemetery; the Jansenists, or "convulsionists" as some called them, provoked such demonstrations of religious zeal openly from 1727 to 1732, when the police closed the cemetery. (They would continue to do so in secrecy until 1760.)

In other times, these events would have resulted in civil war. The condition of the Catholic Church in the 18th century was, however, one of decadence and decline. Recruitment for the priesthood had lapsed, and money for the maintenance and construction of churches was lacking. These troubles were aggravated by the class structure of the clergy, which had produced a definite cleavage between the upper echelons of the religious hierarchy and the general priesthood of more humble origins.

Though civil war did not erupt, riots were common currency throughout the century, be they in reaction to the capture of children for the colonies, taxes, or famine. A poster stuck over the holy water font of a church, in 1768, read: "Pray God for the king who is deaf, dumb, and blind."

Paris in the 18th Century

Paris under the Bourbon kings was decidedly a royal city, as opposed to the Christian city of churches it had been. They—no longer the ecclesiastics—set the style. Among the royal absolutes were art and construction. The Crown took all essential decisions for the piercing of new boulevards, the construction of bridges and squares, the placing of monuments, and the fashioning of the suburbs. The scope of Paris was broadened in all directions: with the extension of the Champs-Elysées, the city stretched in perpendicular splendor from the Pont de Neuilly to Vincennes. This is not to say that the undisciplined and straggling medieval city had been turned into a harmonious classical metropolis. But, for the first time since the Romans, urban organization entered the consciousness of the monarchy and its appointed architects.

The Place de la Concorde, originally Place Louis XV, and the buildings that surround it were designed by Jacques-Ange Gabriel. One of the ingenious aspects of his plan was the opening of the Rue Royale to the north, thereby providing the beginnings of a new north-south link. At the center of that colossal square, the monarch was enthroned astride a stunning stallion and dressed in Roman attire. Parisians reacted by placarding Louis' statue with posters that decried his cowardice, his vices, and his indifference to the plight of his subjects.

Gabriel also designed the Ecole militaire (the Military School), which was built to the west of the city, in a woodland area on the left bank that was still inhabited by wildlife. A large green, known as the Champ-de-Mars, was reserved along the Seine as an exercise field for the military cadets. Madame de Pompadour was the moving figure behind the creation of the academy.

Place de la Concorde. The square, built under Louis XV, would provide the background for the death by guillotine of his son Louis XVI in 1793. Two years later, Place Louis XV was re-christened Place de la Concorde in an effort to efface its association with such events.

Among the other construction projects undertaken during this period were the Royal Library (now the Bibliothèque nationale), the Mint (La Monnaie), the School of Law, and the School of Surgery—all of which were left bank additions, except for the library. A major clean-up was attempted at the Louvre which, at long last, witnessed the gradual destruction of the lean-tos and shacks on its grounds. Notre-Dame was also stripped of myriad attachments blocking the area and was extended by means of a *parvis*, or open square, out front. Similar extensions were envisaged for other churches such as Saint-Sulpice, though all were not completed at the time. Saint-Sulpice and Sainte-Geneviève (now the Pantheon), the two major churches built in the 18th century, were prime examples of the neoclassical design that typified the era. As with many of the public buildings erected then, the architectural concept included squares and avenues that led from them. In contrast to the private mansions that opened inward to courtyards and building facades, these public edifices were conceived to look outward onto the city.

Though France's finances had been totally depleted by the series of wars in which Louis XV had involved the country, leaving the common people penniless, wealth still circulated among an elite intoxicated with the frenzy to build. With the return of the monarchy to Paris at the beginning of Louis XV's reign, the privileged nobility set about building, in particular in an area on the western left bank referred to as the Faubourg Saint-Germain. Major examples of these mostly neoclassical constructions are the Palais Bourbon (now the National Assembly) and the Hôtel de Lassy, both of which were built for one of Louis XIV's illegitimate daughters. The latter is now inhabited by the Speaker of the House of the French parliament.

The Pantheon, commissioned as a church by Louis XV and designed by architect Germain Soufflot, was built on the site of the former Sainte-Geneviève Abbey. It is now the secular resting place of some of France's leading personalities, among them Voltaire, Jean-Jacques Rousseau, Emile Zola, Jean Jaurès, Pierre and Marie Curie, and André Malraux.

Well-heeled merchants, magistrates, professionals, and financiers also built, and they bought titles and connections among the nobility. In addition, they contributed financially to some of the royal projects such as the Place de la Concorde. For their homes, the newly opened areas on the right bank to the west of the Rue Royale and those in the Palais-Royal sector were popular. They vied with the nobility and, since elegance was a must, made ample use of the first-rate Parisian artisans, among the finest in Europe. Interiors remained decorative and ornate in contrast to the simpler, classical lines of exteriors. The aligning of facades and the widening of streets and intersections, in particular for the cutting of new thoroughfares, received due consideration.

Though middle-class housing did not immediately adopt the classical conventions, it did employ architects and often displayed a penchant for rococo design. Rental houses also flourished and reached new heights: six or seven floors in the center of town, and four on the periphery.

Wood disappeared almost completely in the constructions of the era, replaced by weighty stone and limestone rubble. For the first time, in middle- and upper-class homes, rooms underwent specialization. Bedrooms were set apart for sleeping; meals were prepared in a kitchen room; and a room was reserved just for living and dining. Stoves or fireplaces now appeared in most rooms of houses, as did lighting. Each person or couple had their own bed. Bathrooms and inside toilets, however, were generally absent. Only 6.5% of all housing was so equipped.

In the second half of the 18th century, larger buildings increased in number throughout Paris. Apartment houses, schools, and theaters were erected to meet the needs of a growing population, which by then numbered 600,000.

A new wall circled Paris called the Enceinte des Fermiers Généraux, whose placement separated Paris from its suburbs. Its true purpose, however, was taxation: the *fermiers*, or farmers, were tax collectors to whom the Crown "farmed out" the collection of taxes on all merchandise entering the city through its gates. The difference between the sums amassed and the sums due to the king was considered salary.

THE ENLIGHTENMENT

It is called the *Siècle des Lumières* in French, a moniker applied to the 18th century sometime after its demise. What was the Enlightenment, and what made it great? After all, the kings were despots, the government and the administration repressive, the people poverty-stricken, and the country close to bankruptcy.

The power of reasoning was the foundation upon which the Enlightenment rested. It eschewed traditional authority, be it that of the Church or the Crown. Its harbingers of change, though not yet ready to discard the latter, saw in the former the purveyor of superstition and irrational thought. Rational criticism was the Enlightenment's binding characteristic and was applied both to institutions and individual behavior. Although café life had reached new heights and played a role in the events that would culminate in revolution, the Enlightenment's principal vehicle was the salon. High-society women regularly received people of charm, intellect, and station into their homes: writers and artists, professionals, prominent bourgeois, and members of the nobility. They were the so-called philosophers. Men such as Voltaire, Montesquieu, Rousseau, and Diderot were mainstays at these events. Through the contacts that the salons provided, musicians, sculptors, and painters were freed from subservience to a single client—the monarchy.

The publication of Diderot's *Encyclopedia* (1751–1766), which included the writings of some 150 contributors, was instrumental in defining the individual as a rational being, thereby combating absolutism and developing ideas of participation in the governing process. The content was considered subversive, but the standing of those involved provided a protective covering. To quote the king on the subject of writers: "Those people will be the downfall of the monarchy."

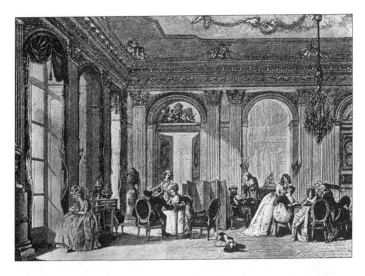

An 18th-century Salon. Forerunner of the club, the salon was an invention of the Marquise de Rambouillet in the early 17th century. It brought together people of wit and distinction with members of the nobility in a setting outside the Court.

Denis Diderot (1713–1784), the materialist and atheist philosopher and writer who founded the Encyclopedia in 1751. It assembled the writings of the leading exponents of 18th-century philosophy and contributed largely to the ideas echoed in the French Revolution.

CHAPTER 7

THE PEOPLE'S FIGHT

THE EVE OF REVOLUTION

Louis XV's last mistress, the Countess du Barry, would attend meetings of the Council of State, seated on the arm of the king's chair, and make funny faces at his ministers. The king was amused. When he died in 1774, he was not mourned. The population's major concern at the time was how to pay for the next loaf of bread.

His grandson, Louis XVI (r. 1774–1791), was just twenty when he received the crown. "We are so young!," he cried. With joy Parisians welcomed him and his ravishing bride, Marie-Antoinette. Unfortunately he was an ordinary fellow, by all accounts a voracious eater and rabid hunter with no interest in art or theater. The hunt was a daily exercise, and he kept statistics on the game he felled. He also enjoyed the locksmith's trade and became quite proficient at it.

Marie-Antoinette was beautiful and frivolous. It seems that Louis adored her, while she had only disdain for him. The marriage between the royal houses of France and Austria was intended to bridge the rift that years of war and rivalry had created. She was a pleasure-seeker and spendthrift; her generosity to herself and her protégés earned her the title of "Madame Déficit." In the final years of the monarchy, the antipathy of the public would be expressed in the more sinister calling of "l'Autrichienne," the Austrian woman. By then both she and the king would be despised.

One of the first acts of the new king was the reinstatement of the old parliament and a modest reduction in the military budget. It soon became apparent, however, that the monarch was not a leader, but a tool of the Court and the queen's allies. Events surrounding Turgot, the man he installed as Comptroller General, are a good illustration of the weakness of the Crown.

Turgot had pledged himself to "no bankruptcy, no increased taxation, no further borrowing." To that end, he called for the free circulation of grain and introduced accounting methods, a budget, and improved management of the royal finances. In 1776 Turgot presented a series of edicts to Louis XVI. One would have abolished forced labor as an alternative to taxation, while another would have canceled the privileges of the medieval guilds. These were radical measures, greeted with hostility by parliament, feudalists, financiers, guild masters, and members of Court, including the queen. When the head of government joined Turgot's detractors, only the king remained. However, to support Turgot and impose the recommended reforms required a willpower that Louis did not possess. He capitulated and dismissed Turgot, nonetheless saying "Only you and I truly love the people."

Other men in positions of power attempted to introduce the reforms necessitated by an ailing system of government. Unfortunately one after another were forced to admit defeat, as the privileged classes were not ready to accept limitations on their feudal rights.

Meanwhile, France continued to be plagued by debt and inflation, which led to unprecedented increases in the price of bread. The rise of grain prices had been general but gradual since 1730. In 1789 they rose by 127%, with the price of wheat increasing by 150% and that of rye by 165% in July alone. While the purchase of bread previously had accounted for fifty-eight percent of the budget of the lower classes, in 1789 this figure shot up to eighty-eight percent.

The significance of these figures is of prime importance in any evaluation of the events of 1789, for the overwhelming majority of the population had no resources for the purchase of anything besides bread. The consequences for the overall economy were devastating. The textile and manufacturing sectors lagged for lack of clientele, and urban unemployment may well have affected half of Paris' population.

The minister of finances paid the French contribution to the American War of Independence by borrowing. The difference between the State's expenditures and its revenues left a deficit of roughly twenty percent, which necessitated still more borrowing. At the same time, the poverty of the population had resulted in less tax revenues in a year of poor harvests, which forced France to import, and to pay increased prices for, grains. The purchasing power of the State was so severely strained that, in 1787, the ministry of finance proposed that a land tax be paid by every landowner—feudal lords, the nobility, and the Church included. The Assembly of Notables, a grouping of aristocrats, met and refused the tax. Louis responded by firing the finance minister.

Thus aristocratic privilege remained a sacred attribute, representing the dividing line between the bourgeoisie (born of the towns or burgs) and the aristocracy, whose standing was based on the possession of land and the feudal system. So rigid was this

Moulin de la Galette, the only surviving windmill of some thirty that once covered the hill of Montmartre. It is said that Louis XVI's government had grain secretly sent from these granaries to Le Havre at a time when the people of Paris were threatened by famine. It was then brought back by ship and sold at outrageous prices as wheat imported from America.

concept that aristocrats entering industry, manufacturing, or commerce were divested of their privileges and subjected to taxation. Contrary to the British and Dutch aristocracies, which led their countries into the industrial age, French noblemen were prisoners of their privileges.

The battle between parliament and the tribunals, on one side, and the king and his government on the other, became vicious during the year 1787. Finally, in 1788, it was decided to call a meeting of the Estates-General, a political body that convened on rare occasions—the last assembly had taken place in 1614. It had a tripartite membership that voted not individually, but by sector: the nobility, the Church, and the bourgeoisie, the latter representing what was called the Third Estate, which amounted to some ninety percent of France's total population, including artisans and the peasantry. May 1, 1789 was fixed as the date of the Estates-General's meeting, which was convened essentially for the purpose of raising money. In the meantime, however, the wheels of the State administration had to continue turning with its coffers empty.

Emotion among the people ran high and, with each turn of events, the ebb and flow was electric. Whatever capital the parliamentary magistrates had garnered by the very act of standing up to the king was quickly diminished when they, joined by the rest of the aristocracy, opposed any increase in the representation of the Third Estate at the meeting of the Estates-General.

Elections for the Third Estate transformed Paris into a hotbed of political activity. Newspapers were created and pamphlets distributed. Clubs were formed, and notebooks of grievances opened. Talk was incessant in the cafés. Every sector of the population became involved. Fear was also present. As revolutionary fervor took hold, and fear led to panic, the people sought arms in self-defense.

The Palais-Royal was considerably transformed by the Duke of Orleans between 1781 and 1784 by the addition of rental houses, shops, and cafés as a money-making scheme. According to one account of the days leading to revolution, the cafés "are not only crowded within but other expectant crowds are at the doors and windows listening with bated breath to the orators who from chairs or tables harangue each his little audience."

THE REVOLUTION

The Estates-General met at the palace in Versailles. Very quickly, the Parisian representatives of the Third Estate dominated the proceedings and elected the astronomer Jean-Sylvain Bailly as their chairman. On June 23, an attempt was made to force that group to leave the assembly hall, whereupon Bailly rose to say: "A nation in assembly cannot receive orders." With these rebellious words, the delegates held their ground. The following day, they were joined by most of the clergy and a significant group of noblemen led by the Duke of Orleans. In defeat, Louis XVI gave orders for twenty regiments of the royal army to begin marching towards Paris.

On July 11, the king fired the head of government, Jacques Necker. The following day, Paris was the scene of numerous clashes between demonstrators and the royal cavalry. That night several armories came under attack. On the 13th, the bourgeois raised a militia called the National Guard. The following morning, crowds of Parisians forced their way into the Invalides and took away 30,000 rifles and a few cannons. They then marched on the Bastille, at the time a munitions depot and prison, and forced the lifting of the drawbridge. The Bastille guards counterattacked and forty were killed. The governor of the Bastille finally capitulated, but was nonetheless beheaded later in the day. The same fate befell the titular head of the city administration, Jacques de Flesselles. These events constituted the death knell of monarchal authority in Paris. Bailly, by acclamation, took over as mayor of the city on July 15th. In Versailles, the delegates commenced the elaboration of a constitution for France.

Paris Versus Versailles

But all was not over. While Louis XVI was prepared to accept the idea of a constitutional monarchy that would eradicate fiscal privilege, he refused to abolish feudalism, the established social order. In the city interminable lines formed outside bakeries, and demonstrators protested against the high cost of basic necessities and for better wages. The situation worsened daily. On October 4, a Parisian newspaper warned of an aristocratic plot to starve the city. The following day, several hundred women embarked on a march to Versailles in order to demand bread. National guardsmen, led by Lafayette, joined the march.

On the afternoon of October 6th, the fearful royal family was escorted to Paris by the National Guard—their bayonets on high, impaling loaves of bread. As the grain-laden wagons traveled towards the city, marchers screamed and jeered: "Back to Paris, the baker, the baker's wife, and the baker's helper."

In the eyes of the French, the 14th of July constitutes a turning point in their history that is significant enough to be recalled each year as a national holiday. Perhaps more far-reaching in import, however, were these events of October 5–6, 1789. For Louis XVI and his family—Marie Antoinette and their two children, Louis-Charles and Marie-Thérèse Charlotte—entered the Tuileries Palace more as prisoners than as house guests. Shortly thereafter, the delegates of the Estates-General traveled back to Paris from Versailles, setting up headquarters and resuming their deliberations at the Tuileries Palace.

Tuileries Castle. Construction on the Château des Tuileries, positioned at the opposite end of the Tuileries Gardens from the Louvre, was begun in the late 16th century; it became the residence of the kings of France until abandoned by Louis XIV for Versailles. During the Commune in 1871, it was set afire and then totally demolished by decision of the Chamber of Deputies.

DEATH OF THE MONARCHY

Once sparked, the fire of revolution blazed forth to engulf the entire country. Throughout France, revolutionary committees were forged. Then the peasants rose. The message that these rural uprisings sent to the Constituent Assembly was clear: no further seigneurial exactions by local lords and ecclesiastics. While the delegates voted to end feudalism and serfdom, their generosity stopped short at what was termed "contractual" feudalism—lands that had been granted to peasants in the past and for which seigneurial dues were collected. According to the bourgeois concept of property, these feudal rights could only be remitted against compensation that few peasants were in a position to pay. Generally speaking, the overriding bourgeois principle was the elimination of all obstacles to economic freedom and expansion, including such "obstructions" as unionizing, striking, and free association.

Lafayette's national guardsmen maintained order in Paris. The needy received succor, and the price of bread dropped. Thousands of army officers and aristocrats—among them, the king's brother—fled abroad. Numerous clubs were formed by elites of different persuasions, from supporters of the monarchy to radical republicans, with some functioning as would a political party. Each clan disseminated the revolutionary watchwords through its own newspapers, handbills, and public readings. The most noted, the Jacobin Clubs, a network of organizations covering all of France, undertook to monitor the administration and denounce counter-revolutionaries. Their power was such that they could summon public officials for hearings. The army also played a revolutionary role, its rank and file identifying with the representatives of the Third Estate. The tricolor cockade—blue, white, and red—became the symbol of the new regime.

Paris was divided into forty-eight sections, each with its own assembly and the ability to petition the National Assembly. In the main, however, Parisians ignored and eschewed the electoral process. Of a voting population of 80,000 citizens, only 14,000 went to the polls for the mayoral election.

The elimination of the monarchy had not been a goal of the Third Estate, nor of the Constituent Assembly. However, at a time when England and Holland had already embarked upon the industrial revolution, leadership was required to advance reforms and modernize a country mired in feudalism and debt. Louis XVI had displayed none of the necessary qualities: while accepting a measure of compromise under pressure, he resisted reform to the bitter end. On June 21, 1791, he became part of a vast scheme to retake the country by force. With the royal family, he secretly left Paris for the purpose of joining counter-revolutionary forces stationed outside the country, along the Rhine. His royal appetite got the better of him, however, and so many stops were made for the extravagance of sustenance that he missed the relays assigned to lead him from one rendezvous point to the next. In Varennes, in eastern France, he was recognized and arrested. Upon his return to the capital, Parisians lined the streets, sullen, disapproving, and hostile. According to a chronicler of the time: "The rooftops were covered with men, women, children; barriers were put in place; the trees were heavy with people. Everyone's hat remained on. The most majestic silence reigned. . . ."

The monarchy was no longer beyond reproach. Revolutionaries, such as Danton and Robespierre, called Louis a traitor and demanded that he be judged. To fill the power vacuum, various political groupings vied with one another. The situation, fraught with danger, resulted in the radicalization of the revolution. The goal was now popular democracy.

Maximilien de Robespierre. Nicknamed the Incorruptible by the people of Paris, his stated goal was a regime of Virtue. He instituted the Terror in an effort to quell the counter-revolution, eventually eliminating his revolutionary rivals Jacques Hébert and Georges-Jacques Danton. He was overthrown and executed in 1794.

The constitution promulgated in September 1791 created a National Assembly that abolished the monarchy and prepared to arm against the counterrevolution. Prussian and Austrian armies, led by relatives of the royal family and bolstered by French émigrés, amassed along France's eastern frontiers. In December Louis XVI wrote to one of his agents: "Instead of civil war, we shall have war abroad and things will be much better."

THE "SECOND REVOLUTION"

Hunger was the cement of the Revolution, uniting the poor and landless. Its leadership was bourgeois, however, which helps to explain the turmoil and confusion of the times. As the internal situation worsened with new inflation and food shortages, deep divisions appeared in what had been the Third Estate. For, as revolutionary fervor intensified, the bourgeoisie became fearful of what they saw as a threat to their economic freedom, wealth, and privileges. New ideological and political groupings developed: the Parisian Sans-Culottes, who represented the common people; the Girondins, who represented the classic bourgeoisie; and the more radical Jacobins and Montagnards, who backed Robespierre.

A "second revolution" occurred on August 10, 1792, when the Girondins were overwhelmed by the people demanding and procuring universal male suffrage and the right to bear arms— the advent of democratic rule. Abandoned by his troops, Lafayette joined the Austrians at the frontier. Then, the trial of Louis XVI and his execution on January 21, 1793, produced a major split within the revolutionary ranks. The Girondins had striven to save the monarch hoping to appease the European powers aligned against the new Republic. Their inclination was towards appeasement with the aristocracy at home as well. In June of that year, they were eliminated from the political scene. The Old Regime had succumbed and the monarchies of Europe were being defied in the strongest possible terms.

THE TERROR

By the summer of 1792, 400,000 men bore arms against counter-revolutionary forces. Led by professional soldiers rapidly promoted to fill the vacuum left by the émigrés, they were successful in battle along the Rhine and in the Austrian Netherlands (today's Belgium), literally saving the Revolution in the fall of 1792. The following spring, however, they suffered a number of setbacks. The military problem required drastic solutions, for increasing numbers of men had to be recruited, equipped, and fed. Money had to be borrowed or printed. As the situation became more chaotic, particularly in the countryside where counter-revolutionary forces had gained momentum, the answer of Robespierre's government was a series of radical measures called the Terror.

The goal of these measures was civil obedience and strong central government. In practical terms the Terror translated into tight economic controls—including a maximum price for grain and particularly severe punishment for speculators and hoarders—and extensive powers to raise armies and provide for the defense of the Revolution. Judicial Terror replaced direct action by the people. The bodies created for the implementation of the Terror were called the Committee of Public Safety, a type of war cabinet, and the Committee of General Security, which oversaw the policing of the country. The Jacobin clubs throughout France served as vehicles for the implementation of the Terror at the local level. Exactions and executions became significant arms of governance. It is estimated that, in Paris alone, some 6,000 people met their death under the guillotine. "Whilst Robespierre reigned, blood flowed and no man went short of bread," a Parisian carpenter commented.

Success of the revolutionary armies, against both their internal and external enemies, was achieved in the fall and winter of 1793. In its immediate wake, however, dissent and factional fighting within the power structure took prominence. The contradictions between the bourgeoisie and the general population sharpened and then became insurmountable. The Terror lasted until the end of 1794, at least in respect to economic measures. By this time Robespierre had been executed, the Sans-Culottes marginalized, and the Jacobin clubs closed. In short, the popular movement had been laid prostrate.

The harvests of 1794 were poor, and the following winter bitter. In the spring of 1795, Parisians rioted to demand a reduction in the price of bread, only to be quelled by the army and the National Guard. The Revolution, which had succeeded with the creation of the National Guard, was now its victim. It had come full circle.

Revolutionary Furor and De-Christianization

One of the very first acts of the Revolution was the destruction of the *Enceinte des Fermiers Généraux*, the tax barrier that separated Paris from its outskirts. After all, what free city could accept the taxation of its citizens upon entering its walls? A second object of particular scorn was the Bastille, which was ripped apart stone by stone. (Its materials were later used for the construction of the Bridge of the Revolution, today's Pont de la Concorde.)

In 1791 the Constituent Assembly, faced with mountainous debts, nationalized the assets and properties of the Catholic Church and put them up for sale. As compensation, the clergy were put on salary. Monastic orders were dissolved, except for those that operated educational institutions and hospitals. Eighteen churches were razed. Orders were issued to behead the statues of what were believed to be the kings of France along the facade of the Notre-Dame Cathedral. They were actually the kings of Judah and were later replaced. (The original heads were discovered in 1975 in a Parisian cellar and are now on display at the Cluny Museum.) The word "saint" was chiseled off street signs, and Place Louis XV was "de-baptized" Place de la Révolution.

A lay, republican calendar was devised to replace the Christian calendar. Divorce was authorized. Although mass and other forms of religious practice were outlawed, on December 6, 1793, the principle of religious freedom was solemnly affirmed and private religious celebrations were authorized.

Numerous works of art, also considered representative of an inglorious and decadent past, might conceivably have been destroyed were it not for the efforts of Alexandre Lenoir. Spending considerable energy and money to purchase—or simply to take— threatened works, he collected them at the Petit-Augustin

The School of Fine Arts, L'Ecole des Beaux-Arts, which warehoused works of art saved from destruction following the Revolution, took over the 17th-century Petits Augustins Church and Convent, depicted here.

Convent, now the School of Fine Arts. (Many of these pieces can be viewed at the Museum of French Monuments.)

To feed the starving capital, potatoes were planted in the Tuileries and Luxembourg Gardens. Clearly, this was not a time for building but the Revolution required space to house its institutions and creations. New schools were set up in temporary quarters and contributed to the prestige of Paris, as well as the centralization of political and economic power. The only area of building that truly flourished in the 1790s was theater. Considered seditious by the monarchy, theaters were authorized without restriction by the National Assembly.

CHAPTER 8

THE RETURN OF AUTHORITARIAN RULE

THE DIRECTORY

By 1795, the people of Paris were politically exhausted and war-weary. The Church's power had been curtailed and the clergy throttled. The aristocracy had been defeated, and feudal rights abolished. The popular movement had been thwarted and muzzled. Peace with Holland, Prussia, and Spain had been secured, though war with Austria was to continue until the latter part of 1797.

The economic situation was disastrous, and the people were crying for food. Parisians had not known such cold, hunger, and misery in nearly a century. It was at this time that the bourgeoisie consolidated their power, with predictable results. Even as hoarding and speculation went unpunished, food riots were quashed with fury, and arrests and banishment were the rule.

In 1795 a third constitution was elaborated. It guaranteed property rights, while eliminating the universal right to primary education and general male suffrage included in the first constitution. The Declaration of 1789 had stated that "men are born free and equal in their rights, and so remain"; this was now superceded by "equality consists in the fact that the law is the same for all." Executive authority was invested in the Directory, a committee of five with defined and separate powers. Under this regime, which would last until 1802, monarchists and the clergy regained some measure of support, while former Jacobin leaders were victimized.

These were years of depression and constant rearrangement of the electoral system to suit the needs of government, to such an extent that the democratic process was undermined. Paris lost its central administration, and the city was divided into separate, more controllable municipalities. The Directory's general tendency was centralization and authoritarian rule from Paris.

War and counter-revolution exploded again at home and abroad in the spring of 1799. While things were brought quickly under control, France's continued economic woes and the Directory's political instability led to an ever-increasing reliance on the army. Thus, the ground was being set for Bonaparte's coup d'état . . . and dictatorship.

The Empire

Napoleon Bonaparte's coup was no ordinary military takeover. Recent elections had replaced the conservatives of the Directory with ex-revolutionaries and neo-Jacobins. The Directory was by then a failure and a new, more stable system of government was a recognized necessity. However, any constitutional change required ten years of procedure. The only alternative was the organization of a coup d'état, for which event General Bonaparte's return to Paris after a series of heralded military campaigns could be deemed providential.

In 1799 the General was named First Consul for ten years and invested with considerable executive power. A plebiscite was then held to "legitimize" this arrangement. So successful was Bonaparte in organizing and policing France that, in 1802, by means of another plebiscite, he was named Consul for life and granted the privilege of naming his own successor. In this way, the electoral process and representative government were bypassed, and the status quo guaranteed. As the administration gained in efficiency so did the regime in dictatorial power.

At the turn of the 19th century, Paris presented the most luxurious and the most miserable of aspects. Certain quarters displayed delightfully refined facades: the Champs-Elysées, surrounded by forest; the Place de la Concorde; and the new Saint-Honoré quarter, the area from there to Montmartre covered now with the plush residences of merchants and generals whose fortunes had been amassed during Bonaparte's Italian campaigns. Beyond the Paris of the affluent, however, municipal services were exhausted. Filth lined the streets, garbage was left unattended, and street lighting was either non-existent or non-functioning. The Luxembourg Gardens, the Invalides, and the Palais-Royal Gardens stood in ruin.

The First Consul presided over the destinies of a city whose population had been reduced by war and abandonment to little more than 500,000 inhabitants. With the naming of a police prefect and of forty-eight police commissioners, one for each neighborhood, Bonaparte was to break the back of the city's political opposition, essentially neo-Jacobin and royalist at the time. He intended Paris to be a showpiece—a capital worthy of France, of Europe, indeed, worthy of himself. Social peace and his endless victories in battle over the monarchies of Europe quelled dissent in the early years.

When a poor harvest and organized penuries of grain gave rise to bread riots and the stampeding of bakeries, imports and new regulations, resembling those of the Old Regime, insured continued supply. To reduce unemployment, no-interest loans were granted to manufacturers. The harvests of 1802–1804 were excellent, and French political and economic domination of Europe contributed to prosperity and social tranquility.

In 1804 Bonaparte held another successful plebiscite, transforming his consulate into an empire. As the site of the coronation, the emperor and empress, Napoleon and Josephine, chose Notre Dame de Paris, which had served as a warehouse for wine and grain since the Revolution. Immense tapestries were hung to conceal the walls in disrepair.

As country after country was overrun, the vanquished paid and France prospered. But when they could no longer pay, the toll in men and money gradually became unbearable. The first major financial crisis in 1805 drew heavily on the finances of the Bank of France, as thousands of Parisians lined the streets demanding coin in exchange for paper bills. In 1806, the manufacturing industry went into a severe slump. Following Napoleon's divorce and marriage to Marie Louise of Austria in

1810—events judged harshly by Parisian workers who had benefited from Josephine's largess—official receptions paled in style. Repression increased as police presence reached extreme proportions intervening in private and in public life. The population no longer submitted tamely to providing human fodder for the Emperor's foreign campaigns.

The beginning of the end of empire and the emperor dates to 1810. Defeat in Spain and rampant speculation and penury were to have catastrophic consequences. In that year alone, 270 firms in Paris and the suburbs went out of business; sixty others followed in January 1811. Major city banks were forced into bankruptcy and unemployment figures rose sharply. Disaster was avoided solely through large, personal orders for furniture and household goods from Napoleon himself, thanks to which Parisian workers would remain loyal to him to the bitter end.

Another poor harvest and another acute bread crisis took their toll in 1811. Though the harvests of 1812 and 1813 improved the people's lot, the Emperor's defeat at Leipzig was to close the door to profitable markets. Then came further defeat in Prussia and Russia and, finally, retreat. Parisians, who had not seen occupation troops since 1594, would soon be defending themselves against an invading force composed of Prussians, Russians, Austrians, and Englishmen. The city was unfortified, undermanned, and its people lacking in arms and training. On March 30, 1814, the attack was launched. Paris surrendered at two in the morning on the following day, and Napoleon was deposed by the Senate two days later. On April 6th, he abdicated and went into exile on the Mediterranean island of Elba.

Backed with the strength of the occupying forces of the European monarchies, Louis XVIII (r. 1814–1824) entered the city and reclaimed the Bourbon crown on May 3, 1814. The bourgeoisie offered allegiance. However, the immediate, forceful return of the Church and rumors that property would be restored to the émigrés and the nobility, added to the English economic blockade and general insecurity, soon prompted the former ruling class of the Revolution and the Directory to withdraw their support. In the meantime, Napoleon landed on the Mediterranean coast and undertook an epic trip through France, gathering force, and then arriving in Paris. He established residence once again at the Tuileries Palace, and remained for what is known as "the hundred days." Then, once again, on June 22, 1815, following his bloody defeat at Waterloo, he bowed his head in abdication. A few scattered voices could be heard crying, "Long live the Emperor!"

This statue by Vicenzo Vela represents a dying Napoleon at St. Helena. The second photo is the statue and column dedicated to his glory, which stands at the center of the Place Vendome.

NAPOLEON'S LEGACY

Napoleon's reign may have been short-lived, but it left an indelible mark on the face of Paris. The *cour carrée* was enclosed to complete the Louvre, and the Carousel arch built and dedicated to the glory of the French armies. Arcades in the Italian manner and new streets developed the monumental character of the city: Rue Castiglione, Rue des Pyramides, and Rue de Rivoli. Cemeteries were laid out at the city limits of the time: Montparnasse, Père Lachaise, and Montmartre. Five new bridges were constructed, including Austerlitz and the Pont des Arts. At the center of the Place Vendôme a spiral column was erected, recounting the feats of Napoleon's 1805 campaigns, at the summit of which he ruled swathed in a Roman toga.

The Church of the Madeleine was completed in the shape of a Graeco-Roman temple, and was also dedicated to the French armies. On the opposite side of the Seine, the Palais-Bourbon received a columned portico to face the Madeleine. The Arch of Triumph at the Etoile was begun, in 1806, in honor of the victories of the Grand Army. High schools were constructed. Houses received numbers. Eight covered food markets were installed around the city, as well as the flower market on the Ile de la Cité and five slaughter houses. "Sire, give them water," he was told and the Ourcq Canal was built and eighty public fountains designed. Not to mention the extraordinary works of art carried off as bounties of war, which adorned Paris and enriched its museums.

In addition to the architectural and cultural legacy of Napoleon's reign, he provided France with its first unified legal system and laid the groundwork of a modern, centralized bureaucracy.

Arcades à l'italienne, the Rue de Rivoli, was commissioned by Napoleon and named for the Italian city where he defeated the Austrians in 1797, during his Italian campaigns.

Quai de Jemmapes. In 1802 Napoleon commissioned a series of canals to connect the Seine to the Escaut and Meuse Rivers and to transport Paris' drinking water. The Quai de Jemmapes on the right bank borders on the St. Martin Canal, which is the last of this series of canals that cover a distance of roughly 75 miles.

THE RESTORATION

Louis XVIII had miraculously disappeared following Napoleon's return to Paris, his entire regime simply melting away. On July 8, 1815, he returned to Paris followed by 300,000 foreign soldiers who would bivouac in and around the city for the next two years, in the Luxembourg Gardens and on the Invalides Esplanade, the Champs-de-Mars, and the Champs-Elysées. A limited form of constitutional monarchy was negotiated and a reactionary, revengeful royalist government was invested. Exercising the power to repress, to exact, and to execute, the first year of Louis' reign was known as the White Terror, whose victims were Jacobins and Bonapartists. The Restoration not only brought back the monarchy, it also signaled the return of the clergy whose influence was particularly offensive to the Parisian bourgeoisie. Upon his death in 1824, a detested and now obese Louis XVIII would be replaced by his brother Charles X (r. 1824–1830), a former libertine become devout.

Intent on reestablishing the monarchy in its pre-revolutionary state, his was a rocky reign. It received its first decisive blow in 1827, when Parisian electors (now reduced to large-scale property holders) voted overwhelmingly liberal. In the streets, the crowds manned barricades and cried "Death to the government," "Death to the Jesuits," and "Death to the bigots." Charles X was single-minded, however, as exemplified by his selection for prime minister in August 1829. Jules de Polignac was an anglophile émigré, an ultra-royalist, and a prince named by the Vatican. As conservative and submissive as was the press of the day, commentary on the naming of Polignac was incendiary. When the Chamber of Deputies informed the king of their refusal to cooperate with the new head of government, Charles X dissolved parliament. On July

27, 1830, orders were issued to muzzle the press. At that point Parisians took to the streets, mounting barricades and manning their rooftops. Soldiers deserted the armed forces sent in to quell the demonstrations and, within three days—thereafter known as the "Three Glorious"—Paris fell to the insurgents. The reign of the Bourbons was thus consummated; but attempts to recreate the Republic were also thwarted as members of the Chamber of Deputies gathered in haste to name the new head of state: Louis-Philippe, Duke of Orleans.

THE JULY MONARCHY

The July Monarchy, as Louis-Philippe's reign was called, is best remembered as a long suite of demonstrations, riots, and insurrectional movements, which were interspersed with political trials and attempts on the sovereign's life. Workers organized and went on strike, demanding a better lot. For the republican opposition, the essential issue was electoral reform, for wealth remained the basis on which the right to vote was granted. By 1833 the Human Rights Society, uniting various republican clubs and associations, covered Paris with 160 sections. An attempted insurrection the following year, although a failure, did give rise to the reorganization of the capital. For the first time since 1794, Paris was granted its own city council.

The July Monarchy's contradictions can be appreciated in the juxtaposition of two events: the erection of a monument on the Place de la Bastille in honor of the Three Glorious days, and the return of Napoleon's remains from exile on the island of Saint-Helena to a magnificent resting place in the Invalides. Gradually the political makeup of the dozen or so Parisian members of the Chamber of Deputies changed, moving further to the left. Republicans dominated and, in 1843, a Socialist was elected from the very bourgeois neighborhood around the Invalides (today's seventh *arrondissement*). Opposition to Louis-Philippe increased in strength as economic problems beset the country once again, and as disclosures of government scandals, corruption, and political payoffs enraged the population.

Against this background, a banquet in favor of electoral reform was organized by the republican opposition. (The banquet system was the means used to circumvent laws forbidding political meetings.) The very day of the banquet—February 22,

1848—the government ordered it banned, whereupon several thousand students and workers took to the streets. King Louis-Philippe called out the National Guard, whose companies not only refused to restrain the demonstrators but marched through Paris with them to cries of "Long live the reform!" and "Down with the Guizot government!" The king immediately dismissed Guizot and named a successor.

In celebration crowds headed for the Ministry of Foreign Affairs on the Boulevard des Capucines, where soldiers guarding the building opened fire, killing 100 demonstrators. The republicans loaded their bodies on a wagon, which they dragged through the streets of Paris demanding revenge. By the morning of February 24, 1848, 1,500 barricades were in place throughout the city. However, the commander of the regular troops renounced any attempt to engage in battle. Later in the day, Louis-Philippe abdicated in favor of his son, the Count of Paris. The people of Paris, however, would not let another opportunity bypass them. They invaded the Chamber of Deputies and demanded the organization of a provisional government. The royal throne was carried from the Tuileries Palace and burned on the Place de la Bastille, site of the monument to the Three Glorious days that had brought the July Monarchy to power.

CHAPTER 9

THE STRUGGLE FOR DEMOCRACY

THE SECOND REPUBLIC

The Republic was proclaimed and radicals had their day, winning universal male suffrage, freedom of the press and assembly, and the democratization of the National Guard. The economy had come to a standstill, however, and workers were demanding guarantees of a better future. Producers' workshops were launched paying a minimum wage, immediately employing 33,000 men. Within weeks the news spread and the numbers rose to 80,000, as the poor arrived from surrounding areas. Nonetheless, commerce continued to flail and the coffers of the State were depleted. In Alexis de Toqueville's words, "Paris was in the sole hands of those who owned nothing. . . ."

Elections for a Constituent Assembly were held in April 1848. On this occasion, universal male suffrage was practiced for the first time in history in a major state. Although political parties were essentially nonexistent, eighty-four percent of the electorate went to the poles. The tendency was to support those with a name, with experience, and with influence, and the result was an Assembly of moderate and conservative republicans. On June

22, it was announced that the National Workshops would be closed. The following day, barricades went up in the poor, eastern neighborhoods of Paris. "Liberty or death" was the cry of the tens of thousands of people ready to die for the right to work. An army of some 100,000 troops set about to quell them. Thousands died, and 12,000 were taken prisoner. Martial law was introduced.

CENTRALIZATION

In the 19th century, success was measured from Paris. It was the intellectual and financial capital of France, as well as the seat of cosmopolitanism and of the best schools. To Paris talent came seeking recognition: Delacroix, Lamartine, Balzac, and Berlioz. Victor Hugo installed himself on the Place des Vosges as though he had been born there.

Paris was also the unrivaled political head of the nation, the purveyor of regimes, from the Revolution of 1789 to the advent of the Third Republic. In its narrow streets, a few mattresses, an overturned cart, and some rocks or cobblestones made for a barricade. Several barricades could spell revolt, and a few hundred could mean insurrection, perhaps revolution for a nation.

In the 1830s the railroad made its appearance and was initially treated as an amusing toy. Then train lines were extended outward through France in six directions—from Paris and back to Paris—and insured the predominance of the hub with its six stations. In 1848 the first "pleasure train" left Paris for Dieppe, thus initiating the Parisian tradition of trekking to the seaside in the month of August. The railroad quickly transformed the French economy, allowing produce from the provinces to arrive in the capital more quickly and with less expense than by coach or boat.

From the Bourbons to the Orleanists, however, no grandiose architectural achievements can be cited. The post-revolutionary sovereigns lacked the resources available to their predecessors, and industrialization had not yet advanced sufficiently to mark the Parisian landscape. The only remarkable additions were the arcades, which served as thoroughfares in a heavily congested city devoid of sidewalks. Making use of iron supports and vaulted glass roofs, these functional arcades housed the only clean, modern shops in the city. They would eventually be replaced by the department store but, from a modern vantage point, they could be seen as the forerunners of the shopping mall.

From 700,000 at the beginning of the Restoration, the population of Paris had increased to one million under Louis-Philippe. "A city of uprooted multitudes" and "a campground of nomads" were among the contemporary epithets bestowed upon the city, which was overwhelmingly male. It had also become, in the first half of the 19th century, a dangerous city where crime and prostitution coursed through the streets, children were abandoned, and promiscuity was the rule. While housing construction lagged behind the population growth, new bourgeois neighborhoods did come into being: Saint-Georges, Poissonnière, Europe, Batignolles, and Beaugrenelle.

THE SECOND EMPIRE

The revolutionary movement had been decapitated. Paris was divested of its elected city council and a governmental commission was installed in its place. On September 10, 1848, during a partial election, the capital elected Louis-Napoleon Bonaparte, Napoleon's nephew, to the Chamber of Deputies. In December he cashiered the illustrious Bonaparte name into the presidency of the Republic, despite press disapproval, a poorly-financed campaign, and no support from a political party.

The economic situation remained stagnant, and cholera struck once again. Subsequent changes in the electoral laws, which barred the poor from the electoral process, reduced the voting population of Paris by two-thirds. The division deepened between conservatives, on one hand, and republicans and socialists on the other. The one-term mandate of the elected prince-president, as Louis-Napoleon was then called, was due to come to an end in 1852, and a second mandate was forbidden under the constitution of the Republic.

However, with the backing of General Saint-Arnaud and 60,000 soldiers, Louis-Napoleon took power militarily on December 2, 1851. He claimed that the times were insurrectional and that his coup d'état was a preventive strike. Actually, the only operation in the offing at the time was being organized by the monarchists, who were caught short. On December 21, a plebiscite provided the coup d'état a semblance of legality. One week later, he took leave of the Elysées Palace and settled in the Tuileries Palace, the home of kings. Another plebiscite in 1852 would reestablish the hereditary Empire.

Napoleon III had a sense of his own destiny. He intended executive power to be strong and without opposition. Government was to be de-politicized, while providing for the basic needs of the population. He exercised power personally, convoking his ministers weekly to discuss his agenda and provide information for the decisions he would take. The former political elite did not rally behind his regime as expected, leading him to complain: "The Empress is Legitimist, Napoleon-Jerome republican, Morny Orleanist. I am myself a socialist. The only Bonapartist is Persigny, and he is mad!"

The Second Empire's early years were productive and prosperous. Aware that the empire was constantly under threat and that it would have difficulty surviving his death, the emperor was determined to transform (and to better control) Paris by implanting new, indelible roots. He budgeted for the improvement of certain slum areas, initiated workers' housing, and set up a pawn service to assist with low-interest loans. In 1853 he named Georges Eugène Haussmann as Prefect of the Seine. With this appointment began the largest urban renewal project the world has ever seen—one that would metamorphose Paris from a congested, essentially medieval city into a metropolis of wide boulevards and open spaces. When the Boulevard de Sebastopol was inaugurated in 1858, Haussmann rejoiced: "It's the disembowelment of old Paris—of the districts of rioters, of barricades—by means of a wide central thoroughfare piercing that impracticable maze of streets from one end to the other. . . ."

The list of districts upon which the axe fell and of the avenues and boulevards created would be too long. Suffice to say that particular emphasis was placed on the right bank, on the areas that surrounded the new railroad stations and on the periphery of the city. Among other achievements were a new sewage system and aqueducts, as well as markets such as Baltard's Les Halles, slaughter houses, and the groundwork for

Garnier's Opera. Squares were laid out throughout the city, and parks were created at its four cardinal points: Buttes-Chaumont, Montsouris, Boulogne, and Vincennes. At the same time, standards were established for the construction of apartment houses, which were limited in height to twenty meters and five floors.

But the period was not without its critics, as no provisions were made for the poor, who were shunted from the center of the city to its outskirts, particularly to the east of the city. As the Lazare brothers put it: "Craftsmen and workers were relegated to veritable Siberias crisscrossed by unpaved, unlit, torturous tracks, devoid of markets, of water, lacking everything . . . Within Paris two cities have been created, very different and hostile: the city of luxury surrounded by the city of poverty."

Indeed, Paris was the pleasure capital for the gentry: music from Offenbach; couture from Worth; drinks at the Café de la Paix and the Café de Madrid; theater at the Palais-Royal; horseback riding in the Bois de Boulogne; dinner at the Pré Catalan; and dancing at the Closerie des Lilas, the Grand Hotel, and Hotel du Louvre.

The working-class population of the Second Empire numbered a half million people, who were employed by 100,000 enterprises. Two hundred thousand more were domestics, and 60,000 concièrges. The world of the poor consisted of an eleven-hour working day, whose earnings were barely enough for a few kilos of bread. Their housing was miserable, with a dozen workers often crammed into one room with six beds. Families lived in unsanitary promiscuity.

Contrary to his uncle's reign, which had become more authoritarian over time, Napoleon III's regime turned more moderate. In 1860 he introduced modifications which, while falling far short of a genuine parliamentary regime, were meant to

Pre-Haussmann Paris. Prior to Haussmann's surgical upheaval, these streets were typical of all Parisian ways and byways.

· RVE · DE · LA · MADONNE ·

Boulevard des Italiens. Haussmann created a number of particularly broad thoroughfares that cut through Paris from east to west, including the above, a busy shopping street near the Opera.

As is usual with innovations on the Parisian landscape, the Opera designed by Charles Garnier provoked considerable controversy when it was inaugurated in 1875. Claude Debussy commented: "It will always resemble a railway station; on the inside, it can be mistaken for a Turkish bath!" While the theatre seats but 2,200 people, its stage can accommodate 450 actors at one time, and there is considerable work space beyond.

improve France's position as a constitutional monarchy. In 1861 criticism targeting Haussmann for the increase in the national debt and for his unorthodox methods of financing led the emperor to grant some measure of budgetary control to parliament.

At the same time, each succeeding election in Paris saw an increase in the number of opposition members in the Chamber. By 1863 nine of the ten representatives from the city were republicans. There followed a rebirth of the workers' movement and the first clandestine trade union section in the Temple quarter.

By 1866 the regime was in decline, and Paris was succumbing to another bout of cholera. As Haussmann's boulevards were opened and lined with row upon row of empty apartment buildings—sorry reminders of the financial failure of the renovation exercise—the disintegration of the authoritarian regime was daily more evident. In 1868 concessions had to be made and the liberty of assembly and of the press were authorized, thus giving the vociferous opposition the means to be heard. Elections in May 1869 gave Parisians the occasion to display their hostility to the regime: 77,000 for, and 234,000 against.

In early 1870, Napoleon III dismissed Haussmann and accepted the introduction of an effective parliamentary monarchy. A plebiscite was organized in order to ask approval of the reforms of the past ten years and, despite a negative vote from Paris, they were overwhelmingly sanctioned. The division between city and countryside had been exaggerated by official propaganda, which decried "the reds" and played on the peasantry's fear of revolution and change. The fundamental issue at hand was thus masked: monarchy versus republic.

Was this to be a new beginning for Napoleon III? It might well have been had he not become embroiled in another foreign military campaign for the purpose of asserting France's dominion over Europe; this, despite the fact that his troops, while competent at repression, were ill-prepared for battle. After the Prussians had made known their intentions to occupy the Spanish throne, the French response was hysterical and war ensued. On September 2, 1870, the emperor and his army were defeated at Sedan. When the news reached Paris that Louis-Napoleon had been taken prisoner, crowds invaded the Chamber of Deputies. Its republican members immediately proclaimed the birth of the Third Republic.

THE COMMUNE

The Third Republic's beginnings were, if anything, chaotic. The realization that the Prussians were advancing on Paris produced two contrary movements: the exodus of 100,000 terrified inhabitants of the city, and the arrival of at least as many other people seeking protection behind Paris' fortified walls. At the same time, the provisional republican government was recruiting and assembling army and national guard units. More than 500,000 mostly untrained men answered the call. Parisians were certain of their own invincibility. Victor Hugo's exhortation was typical of their spirit: "You are three million. Rise up and blow them away!" The two sides met in battle at various points, and it was soon evident that the French superiority in numbers would not suffice. Bismarck and his army of 150,000 men advanced swiftly, and laid siege to the city on September 19, 1870.

He then initiated large-scale artillery attacks and, each day for more than three weeks, 200 to 300 shells struck Paris into submission. On January 26, 1871, a ceasefire was concluded, and a costly and humiliating armistice was signed at Versailles two days later. France was amputated of its eastern provinces, Alsace and Lorraine, and it was required to pay five billion francs in war damages. During the conflict, 3,000 soldiers had been killed; 64,000 civilians had died of malnutrition, starvation, and disease; and 1,000 houses had been partially or totally destroyed.

In February national elections were held, essentially to determine whether or not to continue the war. Paris elected a majority of conservative republicans, and the provinces sent parliament a majority of royalists who had campaigned as "peace" candidates. On March 1, the victorious German army paraded down the Champs-Elysées.

For members of the National Guard, who had fought to defend the city, the formation of a new government headed by the ultra-conservative Adolphe Thiers presaged trouble. Pay to the national guardsmen was stopped, and rents and debts were demanded at advanced dates. Fearing the reaction of a city in which all economic activity was at a standstill, Thiers was determined to disarm Paris. In the early morning hours of March 18, 1871, soldiers were sent to the top of Montmartre in order to retrieve the National Guard's 227 cannons. As the city awoke and perceived the maneuver, inhabitants of the neighborhood surrounded the soldiers and fraternized, whereupon the latter turned their guns against their officers and arrested them. Before the day was out the National Guard had hoisted the red flag on the roof of city hall. The Thiers government and supporters, including army units, withdrew to Versailles. The Commune, as the revolutionary municipal authority was called, would survive for two months.

The communal idea was, in fact, the outcome of the temporary authority exercised, during the siege, by the mayors of the administrative districts or *arrondissements* of Paris under the chairmanship of the central mayor, Jules Ferry. Their success in independently administering the city under harsh circumstances was recognized even by Parisian moderates. As the communal idea was elaborated following the creation of the Commune, it intended that every commune of France exercise full autonomy in a federalist France. A salient point of the program was the formation of a National Guard which would be composed of all valid voters, and to which the guard of Paris would be entrusted exclusively.

On April 2 the first battle between the Versaillais and the Communards took place. The imperial army entered Paris on May

21, and the so-called "bloody week" followed. Thiers' soldiers—freed from German prison camps for the battle—are remembered as particularly savage. The fight was waged from barricade to barricade, from house to house and street to street. In all, 20,000 Parisians were killed—or assassinated upon surrendering— and 38,000 arrests were made.

From the outset, the Commune had had little chance of survival, surrounded as it was by a conservative countryside fearful of Parisian radicalism. Its defeat spelled the end of 19th-century revolutionary insurrection. Future generations of militants and revolutionaries would study the Commune experience closely, however, notably among them Marx, Lenin, and Mao Tse-tung.

THE THIRD REPUBLIC

In the wake of the Commune, the prerogatives of the people of Paris were curtailed (and would remain so for another century). The principle of an elected municipal council was maintained, but the council was endowed with only limited authority. In reality, the city would be governed by a prefect of the Seine and a prefect of police designated by the national government. The mayors of the *arrondissements* would be named by the head of State.

In 1873, the National Assembly resolved to erect the Sacred Heart Basilica (Sacré Coeur) as a monument of atonement to expiate the sins of the Commune. It would be situated atop Montmartre for all to contemplate. The radical leader on the city council, Georges Clemenceau, vented the anticlericalism of Parisians in opposing a project for which a public subscription would be opened without municipal consent. The conflict over Sacré Coeur would continue into the 1880s to no avail, just as the municipal council would repeatedly demand jurisdiction over the city's police force and the suppression of the prefecture of police, also to no avail. Finally, the funeral procession of Victor Hugo on June 1, 1885 attended by 800,000 people, belittled the clergy into turning over the Sainte-Geneviève church to the State, which would receive the author's remains in what is now the secularized Pantheon.

In the following years, between 1889 and 1895, socialism forcefully erupted on the Parisian scene. Workers' demands were expressed in numerous strikes, and the first May Day celebrations were organized in 1890. Beginning in 1893, socialist deputies formed a leading block in the National Assembly.

Another major issue, which would occupy center stage from the mid-1880s until the First World War, was the desire for

ONTMARTRE ET LE SACRÉ-COEUR

Sacré Coeur. The pillars of the Basilica plunge 125 feet into the hill of Montmartre, thus avoiding the cavities left by old mine shafts. Its Savoyard bell weighs close to 40,000 pounds; it is one of the largest ever cast and literally exhausted the 28 horses that hauled it to the top.

revenge against Germany. From 1886 to 1889, General Georges Boulanger played the role of figurehead for the nationalist movement, first as minister of war, and later as member of the National Assembly. At the time of his overwhelming victory for a seat in parliament, the Parisian crowds demanded that he let them march him into the Elysées Palace. Fortunately, his sense of responsibility was sufficient to reject the offer: "Why should I conquer power illegally when I am certain to arrive there in six months by the unanimous voice of France?" However, his saga ended shortly thereafter in a most unexpected fashion. Upon being told that a warrant for his arrest had been issued, he skipped town with his mistress and settled in Brussels.

Whatever its outcome, "Boulangism" proved that Paris, while still the center, was no longer the sole determinant of French politics. It was also evidence that Parisians might be republicans today and "boulangists" tomorrow, attracted to authoritarian leaders.

The nationalist movement also brandished, in the closing years of the 19th century, strong anti-Semitic views. The Dreyfus Affair was a case in point, and it would become a cause célèbre. On January 5, 1895, Captain Alfred Dreyfus, a Jew, was accused of transmitting military secrets to the Germans and was condemned to banishment for life. The affair became national with the publication of Emile Zola's "J'accuse," which denounced the investigators' use of false documents to condemn Dreyfus, in Clemenceau's daily newspaper (L'Aurore). Dreyfus was eventually exonerated and the leaders of the nationalist and anti-Semitic organizations arrested, tried, and condemned.

In the early years of the 20th century, confrontation between progressives and nationalists would characterize Parisian politics. Finally, in 1912, the former gained the upper hand.

LA BELLE EPOQUE

In the 1880s and 1890s, Paris experienced a building boom. L'Ecole des Beaux-Arts was churning out classical-style architects, who built decorative residential buildings for a wealthy clientele. Another mainstay of the Beaux-Arts graduates were buildings for the international exhibitions hosted by Paris between 1867 and 1914. This was a period of imperialist expansion and a number of structures were inspired by African or Islamic colonial design. All would be flattened at the close of the exhibitions, however, as Parisians saw them not as enlarging their horizons but rather as outsiders' desire to present themselves on the stage of the great city. For the exhibitions, architects allowed their imaginations considerable leeway. Among their creations were the Galéries des Machines and the Eiffel Tower, as well as those monuments to steel and glass: The Grand Palais and the Petit Palais, which passed the test of permanency following the 1900 exhibition.

Except for the exhibition structures, industrial age architecture and design had been absent from Paris—any departure from classicism was taken as un-French—until *art nouveau* became fashionable for a very short period at the turn of the century. The 1900 exhibition coincided with the opening of the first metro line, for which Hector Guimard was commissioned to design the entrance canopies. The style became symbolic of Parisian modernity but, in 1905, *art nouveau* lost favor as it was considered "foreign" (Belgian) and a break with the past.

The epitome of Parisian architecture at the turn of the century was the Gare d'Orsay, now the Musée d'Orsay. This was also the age of luxury hotels such as the Claridge and the Lutetia, and of the department store: Au Printemps, Les Galeries Lafayette, and La Samaritaine, which followed on the earlier creation of the Au Bon Marché.

Eiffel Tower. Originally castigated as "useless and monstrous" by 300 French personalities, including Guy de Maupassant, Charles Garnier and Alexandre Dumas son, the Tower has become the symbol of Paris. Following its construction for the Universal Exposition of 1889, it was visited by everyone from Queen Victoria to Thomas Edison and Mahatma Gandhi.

The turn of the 20th century will also be remembered as the era in which Paris was consecrated as the world's fashion capital. During the universal exhibition of 1900, twenty fashion designers presented their models on wax mannequins. Their workshops were located around the Place Vendôme and the Grands Boulevards.

Since the middle of the 19th century, the impressionist painters had been stubbornly pursuing a vision of art that the Second Empire's Director of Beaux-Arts damned as "the painting of democrats, of those men who never change their underwear, who wish to impose upon the worldly; it's an art that displeases and disgusts me." In 1894 the painter Gustave Caillebotte's impressive art collection, willed to the State, was refused. The collection included eight Monet, eleven Pissarro, two Renoir, three Sisley, and two Cézanne paintings.

However, by 1900, the year nineteen-year-old Pablo Picasso arrived in Paris, the impressionist painters were represented in city galleries. They had somehow survived the opprobrium of early industrial society. In opposing truth to artificiality, to beauty for beauty's sake, these artists—themselves products of France's bourgeoisie—would achieve consecration in the first decades of the 20th century, and would be acclaimed by that very same society of detractors.

Some time after the "war to end all wars," the period from the turn of the century to the First World War was baptized *La Belle Epoque*. The term was primarily an expression of nostalgia for a bygone world in which Paris was the center, where everything "happened" from the airplane to literature and art. Forgotten was the muck, the blemishes, and the misery. *La Belle Epoque* signified Paris eternal.

CHAPTER 10

THE TWO WORLD WARS

WORLD WAR I

The propaganda machine had, for a number of years, been inciting the population to war. So intoxicating was the nationalist message that, when mobilization was finally ordered on August 1, 1914, it was received with overwhelming enthusiasm by Parisians from the right to the left. Less than one percent of those called up for duty reneged. Within a month, however, reality struck with the arrival of a trainload of haggard, bereft Belgian refugees fleeing the war zone. Then, on August 30, the first German bombs fell on the city. Three days later, the French government packed up and left for Bordeaux. Thirty-five percent of the population joined the exodus to the countryside.

With the men gone to war, women took their place in trade and commerce. They worked in armament factories, substituted in the schools and hospitals, and, as one woman journalist commented, "those who have always refused them the right to leave man's protective shadow are now declaring that the nation needs them in order to survive." But despite women's contributions, the labor force required even more able bodies. In 1916 foreign workers—Chinese, Indochinese, and North Africans—

were imported. Among them was Chou en-Lai, the future Chinese prime minister, who was employed by Renault, the automobile manufacturer whose Parisian factory was turning out tanks.

As the situation worsened, taxation and rationing were introduced. The winter of 1916–1917 was particularly harsh and coal was in short supply, for the Germans had occupied the northern mining regions. Patriotism waned and, in 1917, shouts of "Down with the war!" erupted at the May Day celebrations. Later in the month, thousands of women seamstresses went on strike for better wages and working conditions, sparking a wave of strikes throughout the garment, banking, and armament industries. Cries of "Give us back our husbands" could now be heard.

In 1918 the aerial bombing of Paris intensified and the first Big Berthas struck the city, one of which hit the Saint-Gervais church during mass, killing eighty-eight people. The Germans were a scant forty miles from the city. Their onslaught was broken, however, by an Allied effort involving fresh American troops. Paris was saved.

An armistice was signed on November 11, 1918. By then Parisians were also being devastated by an outbreak of the so-called Spanish flu, which took the lives of 300 to 500 people a week until February 1919.

The Interim

The Great War left France maimed. The country suffered the highest percentage of war dead of any of the belligerents. Those crippled and gassed required assistance. Jobs had to be created for the millions of returning veterans, and war industries had to be converted to peacetime pursuits. A placement agency was opened in Paris.

In April 1919, the eight-hour day and the 48-hour week were voted. Strikes were nonetheless numerous, spirited by the communist-oriented CGT trade union (Confédération générale du Travail). Prices rose and the first consumers' league was founded in the eighteenth *arrondissement*, followed by others throughout the city. The winter of 1919–1920 was severe and coal was still at a premium.

The war had exacerbated nationalist sentiment and reflexes that would be echoed in the December 1919 elections, won on the national and city level by the conservative National Block. On the strength of that victory, the management sector proceeded to dismiss trade unionists and their membership *en masse*. Twenty thousand railway workers were laid off in addition to thousands of industrial workers. Union membership lapsed and, in the succeeding years, unions would be able to exercise little social or political leverage. The municipality did nonetheless set up a series of crèches to assist working women and, in 1923, authorized a large-scale loan for projects to house low-income families called "moderate rental housing" (HLM).

The Communist Party slowly gathered strength in the capital, and Parisians elected Jacques Duclos and Albert Fournier to the National Assembly in 1926. Bitter and often brutal union agitation for recognition were characteristic of the twenties. As a result of changes in the electoral laws and gerrymandering, however, moderates and conservatives were returned to power at each succeeding election.

The twenties were also years of economic gloom, incompetent administrations, heavy borrowing, corruption and, finally, scandals. All of these factors favored the emergence, in the early 1930s, of fascistic organizations on the model of Hitler or Mussolini. Similar support for an authoritarian regime were expressed in the calls for morality in government that emanated from the nationalist and clerical right. When another conservative government, headed by Edouard Daladier, was brought to power in January 1934, cries for "a government of honest people" were widespread. This appeal set off a series of events that culminated, on February 6, in a march on the National Assembly by a crowd of 40,000 demonstrators composed mainly of right-wingers. The policed counterattacked, leaving fifteen dead and hundreds of wounded.

The demonstration of February 6 is significant in that it became the catalyst for the hardening of political lines between the extreme right and the extreme left. As Maurice Thorez, secretary general of the Communist Party, expressed it: "Between the fascists and ourselves, the revolutionary proletariat, a race had begun for the conquest of the middle classes." At the same time, the first indicators of an approaching international conflict were being observed. On May 14, 1935, exercises in civil defense were organized in Paris.

In mid-1935, the radicals, socialists, and the communists joined together in an unprecedented united front in preparation for elections the following year. On July 14, their contract was sealed with an impressive march of 500,000 Parisians from Place de la Bastille to Place de la Nation. The coalition was victorious, and the first Popular Front government was formed on June 6, 1936. Presided over by Léon Blum, a socialist, the regime was supported by the Communist party though they did not participate. In the meantime, however, the first sit-down strikes in France had been initiated, involving more than one million workers. Blum immediately introduced legislation for the forty-hour week, paid vacations, and collective bargaining.

On June 18, the various fascist leagues were officially dissolved, although they would reappear under different guises. Notable among this group were the French Popular Party and the French Social Party, formerly the Cross of Fire (*Croix-de-Feu*), which boasted over a million members in 1937.

The Popular Front was soon weakened by internal dissension between socialists and communists, as well as by strikes, general disorder, and increasing economic decline. In April 1938, with the resignation of the second Blum government, the Popular Front expired.

In the wake of the Blum resignation, Daladier was once again named prime minister. When he returned from Munich with the British prime minister Neville Chamberlain in September 1938, he was given a hero's welcome. To quote Léon Blum: "War has probably been averted. But in conditions such that I . . . can feel no joy . . . and am torn between cowardly relief and shame."

Throughout France, strikes and violent social actions continued to rage. War was coming and the French right was not displeased at the prospect of Nazi Germany barring the route to social revolution in Europe. In Paris only minimal preparations for war were undertaken, beginning in March 1939. Twelve miles of trenches were dug as shelter in the event of aerial bombings; gas masks were distributed; and anti-air raid shelters were opened.

On September 1, 1939, Hitler invaded Poland.

THE HOLLOW YEARS

Following the First World War, private building for the middle class barely survived. The wealthy built in the west end and the immediate western suburbs, such as Neuilly and Saint-Cloud. Their residences and public buildings mixed styles, including art deco, modern design, and a particularly French sort of neoclassicism. The result was unprecedented variety, encouraged by the arrival of a number of foreign architects, notable among them the Swiss-born Le Corbusier. Architectural lines were simple and forms geometric. The new Palais de Chaillot and Palais de Tokyo (Museum of Modern Art) were typical of what is known as stripped neoclassical, or devoid of the decorative aspects of conventional classical architecture. The spate of churches and cinemas built between the two wars in Paris and the immediate suburbs allowed architects a measure of fantasy in their approach. A major endeavor by the city were the unimaginative brick housing projects designed for the gateways to Paris, along the exterior boulevards. A grand project for a "triumphal way" (*voie triomphale*) to link the Champs-Elysées, which had become the most fashionable and modern street in Paris, and the unconstructed Défense was designed. But it was ultimately abandoned for lack of funds.

In the twenties—*les années folles*—fortunes changed hands. Old money petered out and was replaced by that of arms dealers and manufacturers, speculators of all sorts who became the clientele of the *haute couture* houses of Worth, Poiret, and Lanvin. In the thirties, hard times fell on the fashion industry, despite the arrival of new talent exemplified by Chanel, Patou, Balenciaga, and Ricci.

Those "crazy years" saw Josephine Baker, the African-American music-hall vedette, take Paris by storm. Ex-patriot painters and writers from East and West formed art colonies in Montmartre and Montparnasse: Anais Nin, Brassaï, Nabokov, Joyce, Fitzgerald, Hemingway, Miller, and Sylvia Beach. Gertrude Stein dubbed her American compatriots of Paris the "lost generation," those whose ideals had been destructed in the maelstrom of war.

In the thirties André Malraux wrote *The Human Condition*. At the other end of the political spectrum were André Brasillach and Louis-Férdinand Céline, author of *Voyage to the End of the Night*. (During the Second World War, two influential French writers would capture the Parisian public's attention: Jean-Paul Sartre and Albert Camus.)

The inter-war period, referred to by Eugen Weber as "the hollow years," bore witness to a society in flux. Class mobility had accelerated to such a degree that, in a city becoming gradually bourgeois, the traditional 19th-century *haute* bourgeoisie was barely distinguishable. The potentially powerful working population, relegated to the peripheral neighborhoods of Paris, and more and more to its suburbs, achieved only limited social gains despite the Popular Front.

World War II

As of September 1, 1939, Paris' street lights were extinguished, sandbags lined the entrances to public places, and its children were evacuated to the countryside. Restrictions on the sale of meat were introduced, as well as gas rationing. In February 1940, ration cards were distributed. This period of waiting was the "phony" war, during which France bided time behind the Maginot Line while Germany absorbed Poland. The German armies circumvented the Maginot Line, through the Ardennes, and invaded France on May 10, 1940. In June the French government, headed by Paul Reynaud, left Paris for Tours. Roughly two-thirds of the population of Paris followed suit, with approximately two million people moving southward. It was called the "exodus," a slow, desperate, hallucinating march of families along roads littered with broken-down cars, abandoned clothes, furniture, and prized possessions. All the while, the Germans rained bombs down upon them.

On June 14 the first German soldiers entered Paris and, by the end of the afternoon, the German flag floated atop the Arch of Triumph. Nine days later, from the platform of the Palais de Chaillot, Hitler savored the Nazi victory.

In general, the reaction of Parisians to the occupation was one of apathy and passive acceptance. They had been let down by their leaders, by the so-called invincible army, and even by those who had fled the city. Eyewitnesses recall people crying in the streets, others turning their heads to the wall, but also groups of idlers entering into casual conversation with German soldiers. Parisians gradually returned and, by January 1941, they were two and one-half million people in the city.

The crucial problem was survival. Rationing and food lines became synonymous with the occupation. Ersatz products for shoes, wine, coffee, tobacco, and soap were devised. Gas and coal were rationed but, like everything else, could rarely be found. Bicycle "taxis" made their appearance. Subway trains were infrequent and always packed. For those who could afford it, there was the black market.

Paul Reynaud had favored the capitulation of the French army, which would have allowed France to continue the fight against Germany from elsewhere in its empire, presumably North Africa. On the other hand, Philippe Pétain, the 84-year-old deputy prime minister, demanded negotiations and an armistice. Reynaud resigned in defeat, and Pétain signed an armistice according to which Paris came under the direct authority of the Reich. From the seat of the wartime government, the resort town of Vichy in central France, Pétain named the members of a rubberstamp city council that met once a year. For the most part, French administrators remained at their posts.

Pétain was a revered war hero of the First World War, who was responsible more than any other single individual for the lack of preparedness of the French army. An advocate of strong, centralized government, the watchwords of his "nationalist revolution" were "work, family, homeland" (travail, famille, patrie), which were meant to replace the motto of the French Revolution "liberté, fraternité, égalité." His vision of France was that of a country led by an elite dedicated to social harmony and order. That elite would be protected by the continued elimination of working- and peasant-class children from high school (lycée) and university education. The role of women as mothers and housewives was glorified and efforts were made to reduce the number of women at work outside the home. The Pétain regime's declared enemies were the teaching profession, free masons, communists, and Jews. Catholic officialdom sanctioned the regime throughout, content with its support of "morality," family, and religious education. As late as June 1944, the Church denounced the French resistance movement, labeling its members "terrorists."

Jews were excluded by the Vichy government from most professions—law, medicine, and business—and were dispossessed of their holdings. In 1942 the Nazi chief Eichmann ordered the deportation of 100,000 French Jews, whereupon the French police rounded up 13,000 Jews in a Parisian indoor sports arena, the Vélodrome d'Hiver, for shipment by train to Auschwitz. The arrests continued into 1943 and 1944. It is estimated that 43,000 Jews from Paris and the suburbs—or approximately half of the Jewish community—were arrested and deported, of which 34,000 died.

One of the first groups of partisans in Paris was constituted at the Musée de l'Homme (Museum of Man) by a group of intellectuals who published the first issue of *Résistance* in December 1940. The following month, they were denounced and arrested. Following Hitler's invasion of the Soviet Union, in mid-1941, the communists stepped up their activity and soon commanded the largest and most active resistance movement. A cycle of attack and savage repression developed, which prompted General Charles de Gaulle to criticize the armed attacks as "not contributing to the safeguard of Paris." A member of the French government at the outbreak of war, de Gaulle had refused to be part of the Pétain Vichy government and denounced it. Leaving France for London, he then fought to organize what would be called the Free French. In the latter part of 1943, the Parisian Liberation Committee was formed as an umbrella coalition of the various resistance groups, of which the most substantial were communist-run.

The Allies landed in Normandy on June 6, 1944. The FTP (Franc-Tireurs et Partisans) and FFI (French Forces of the Interior) immediately launched preparations for insurrection in Paris. The task before them was gigantic. Perhaps 30,000 partisans with 1,500 rifles and handguns, as well as four machine guns, would face an occupying force of 20,000 well-armed soldiers. The resistance attacked on August 19, striking small groups of German soldiers, confronting tanks, and occupying public buildings. Their charge had little effect, however, until 2,000 policemen made a last-minute decision to aid them in taking the Prefecture of Police. By August 24 they dominated in the street, though they would not have been able to hold the city against a concerted German counterattack.

General Eisenhower, who had planned to bypass Paris rather than be trapped in a house-to-house fight inside the city, then gave orders for Leclerc's armored division to intervene. The German commander, General von Choltitz, took the decision to surrender, explicitly contravening Hitler's orders to fight on and destroy the French capital. On August 26, 1944, de Gaulle marched down the Champs-Elysées surrounded by cheering crowds. Despite bombings on that very day and others thereafter, including a missile attack on September 3, Parisians were delirious. Paris had been liberated.

RECONSTRUCTION

Reconstruction was a gargantuan task. One-quarter of the nation's wealth had been destroyed, as compared to one-tenth during the First World War. The infrastructure was in a state of collapse. Food was scarce and the country was broke, a situation exacerbated by France's entanglement in a costly, ignominious war against national independence in Indochina.

Archaic and suffering, the economy required modernization that led to State intervention. Among the measures taken was the nationalization of gas and electric utilities, a number of large banks and insurance companies, and the Renault automobile firm, which had collaborated with Germany. To quote de Gaulle, the industrial bosses had "disqualified" themselves.

The Third Republic met its death by popular referendum on October 21, 1945, at the same time as delegates to a Constituent Assembly were elected. Women voted for the first time. One year later, another referendum approved the Fourth Republic's constitution of a bicameral legislative system, with the Senate and president of the republic exercising minimal power. Until 1947, when the Cold War forced the communists into opposition, the first postwar governments were coalitions of Communists, Socialists, and Christian Democrats. The Communist Party was then the largest in France, and most observers believed it capable of engineering a coup. Stalin was reluctant to buck the Western powers, however, needing time to complete the Soviet takeover of Eastern Europe.

In 1947 de Gaulle, who had resigned as President of France the year before, made his reentry into partisan politics with the founding of the Rassemblement du Peuple Français (RPF). He based his campaign on the need to create a strong government and a united bulwark against social revolution. In the municipal elections of October 1947, his party won fifty-two out of ninety seats on the Paris city council. The general's brother, Pierre de Gaulle, was elected chairman.

For the resistance movement, liberation was meant to culminate in profound social renewal. But the pre-war coalition disintegrated rapidly, as the electoral body moved from the extreme left to center right. The high hopes entertained for the post-war period were dampened by a return to patterns of social and material injustice inherited from the past. In 1948 the United States released large-scale aid under the Marshall Plan, which contributed to an easing of social tensions.

By 1951 de Gaulle's RPF was in decline, and the municipal elections of 1953 confirmed its demise. Economic recovery was gradual, with consumerism being promoted even as the national debt continued to mount. The cost of the war in Indochina added to the budgetary morass. Inflation was constant, resulting in rising prices with which salaries did not keep pace. Trade unions were active and strikes frequent. Coalition governments were created and overturned at amazing speed, rarely holding office for more than six months. Paris had become a poorly-maintained and gray city, on the periphery of which sprouted appalling shanty towns.

On May 7, 1954, the French army was defeated at Diên-Biên-Phu and forced out of Vietnam. In November of that same year, France embarked on another colonial misadventure in Algeria, which would last for over seven years and ultimately bring down the Fourth Republic.

CHAPTER 11

POST-WAR POLITICS AND CHANGE

DE GAULLE'S RETURN

The conflict in Algeria came to dominate French politics. As of 1951, rousing demonstrations of thousands of Algerian workers during the Paris May Day parades reflected their refusal of their status as exploited, colonial non-citizens. In 1953, during Bastille Day celebrations in Paris, the violence of a police attack against Algerian demonstrators left seven dead and hundreds of wounded on the streets. When war followed at the end of 1954, the drama played out in Algiera as well as in Paris' political arena. Never in agreement on Algerian policy, governments were overturned one after another. Throughout the war, the *pied noir* European settlers, colonial advisors, conservative politicians, and an officer corps determined to compensate for the humiliating defeat in Vietnam exerted considerable pressure.

In May 1958, the Christian Democrat Pierre Pflimlin, known to favor negotiations with the Algerian National Liberation Front (FLN), was called upon to form a new government. Parisians reacted by rocking the capital with massive, acrimonious demonstrations for and against *Algérie française*. On May 13, a group of generals, among them Massu and Salan, took the dramatic step of assuming power in Algeria. They occupied the island of Corsica and elaborated plans for a military takeover of metropolitan France. Paratrooper units were to land on the outskirts of Paris and advance on the capital, in conjunction with military and right-wing paramilitary groups inside France. Civil war seemed imminent until June 1, when de Gaulle, pledging to respect republican institutions, was granted exceptional powers for a six-month period.

De Gaulle had a vision of France as the capital of Europe and a primary world power, which role required modernization of the economy and the military establishment. While at first championing the cause of French Algeria with equipment and men—two million Frenchmen fought in the conflict—he gradually moved towards negotiation with the FLN. This festering burden ill-suited his goals. It had turned Paris into a wartime city once more, with police patrols, public buildings guarded with submachine guns, the torture of Algerian suspects in local commissariats, and angry demonstrations and counter-demonstrations. Diehards of the Secret Army Organization for French Algeria (OAS) ignited a series of bomb attacks in the city, while the FLN struck at strategic targets such as suburban gas reservoirs.

On October 17, 1961, a major demonstration by an unarmed Algerian community was countered, in the center of the city, by the savagery of an unbridled police force. Literally hundreds of Algerians were killed, and their bodies thrown into the Seine. In August 1962, de Gaulle narrowly escaped assassination at the hands of the OAS.

The 1958 constitution for the Fifth Republic was tailor-made for de Gaulle: a presidential regime that enjoyed extensive executive power. His disdain for parliamentary democracy was revealed in the limited powers accorded to the new Chamber of Deputies. The electoral system, instituted by presidential decree, was meant to ensure that the right would henceforth dominate French politics. In reality, it led to the elimination of the center parties and the increased polarization of the left and the right.

During the late fifties and the sixties France industrialized. Centralization was once again emphasized with industrial enterprises encouraged to locate in the Paris region. The immediate response to the enormous influx of population from the provinces was an increase in State-financing of cheap (and very ugly) apartment buildings and housing projects. Finally a plan was devised for the creation of new towns (*villes nouvelles*) outside the city limits, referred to as "dormitory towns." The transfer out of Paris of the working population was an essential part of this plan, with its attendant political consequences. The base of the Communist Party was shifted to what would be called the "red belt," whereas Paris would pursue its gentrification.

A small number of prestige schemes were undertaken in the fifties: the UNESCO headquarters in 1958; the French national radio headquarters, begun in 1956; and the exhibition hall at the Défense, completed in 1959. In the early sixties the old city building codes were revised to allow for greater upward construction. For the central *arrondissements*, I through XII, changes in regulations concerning height were scant. The rest of Paris underwent drastic changes, however, approaching the magnitude of Haussmann's earlier transformation of the city. Entire quarters were destroyed, clearing the way for promoters and speculators to create buildings of dubious quality and design, known as International Style.

MAY '68 REVOLT

In March 1968, on the drab, unappealing university campus at Nanterre on the outskirts of Paris, a small group of leftist organizations protested against the inadequacies of the educational system, as well as against the war waged by the United States in Vietnam. The demonstration was brutally repressed, engendering new protests in Paris. The police intervened against demonstrators at the Sorbonne and, on May 6, engaged in fierce street battles in the Latin Quarter, leaving 800 students wounded. The first barricades went up in the Rue Gay-Lussac on May 10. Having secured trade union backing, workers marched alongside students in a gigantic protest parade through the streets of the left bank. By May 20, strikes and work stoppages throughout the country, involving some ten million workers, closed France down.

The events had all the marks of a 19th-century revolution, this time against authority—parental as well as official—against elitism, existing institutions, and an educational system still based on exclusion. Faced with the continuing prospect of politicians and practices inherited from past regimes, the coming generation revolted. The government and the establishment were taken by surprise, unprepared for such vehemence and reprobation. But they soon rallied, and made a few gestures towards the trade unions. De Gaulle announced the dissolution of the National Assembly and new elections, denouncing those who had sought his downfall. This statement was aimed as much at politicians such as Pierre Mendes-France and François Mitterand, who had offered to head a progressive front government, as at the students, trade unions, and radical political parties. By mid-June the barricades had been dismantled. Few political or material gains had been realized. Social relationships and mores, however, would never be the same.

From de Gaulle to Giscard d'Estaing

In 1969 de Gaulle's proposals for "participation"—essentially cosmetic modifications presented as a program to increase worker involvement in industry as well as regionalization—were refused by fifty-three percent of the population. De Gaullian logic required that he resign. Candidates for his succession were not lacking, among them were Georges Pompidou, his former prime minister, and Valéry Giscard d'Estaing, the former finance minister.

Pompidou continued roughly the same policies as de Gaulle, emphasizing modernization and the fight against inflation. He prized himself on his knowledge of modern art and architecture, with his tastes leaning towards towers, speedways, and urban renewal. The project which his name graces—the Pompidou Center—provoked considerable controversy. It appears that Pompidou himself was not delighted with the design by Renzo Piano and Richard Rogers but acceded to the choice of the selection committee. After Pompidou's death in 1974, the newly elected president, Valéry Giscard d'Estaing, considered discontinuing the project but construction was too advanced. It remains the only example of the Modern Movement in Paris; even the apartment housing units created later to the north of the Center, rather than integrate with it, adopted an uninspired, neo-medieval style.

The de Gaulle and Pompidou years enjoyed unprecedented prosperity. Although the standard of living improved measurably, discontent was still widespread since the new wealth was unevenly distributed and the emphasis placed on controlling inflation meant that budgetary expenditures for education, health, and public housing were kept to a minimum. Just as Giscard d'Estaing took over from Pompidou, the economy took a steep downturn. Inflation rose to over fifteen percent and the rate of economic growth fell abruptly. His remedy was a reduction of the national deficit and of government expenditures. The problem of unemployment was not addressed, however, so the number of jobless continued to rise, even as the rate of inflation gradually ebbed.

Giscard introduced a new style in the presidential office with less emphasis placed on formality and with legislation adapted to the more liberal moral standards. The voting age was reduced to eighteen; abortion was legalized; divorce laws were simplified; and programs were adopted to make secondary education available to a wider range of students. In the last years of his mandate (the presidential term was seven years at the time), inflation and unemployment rose sharply. These economic concerns were compounded by several scandals involving the president personally, in particular one concerning diamonds from Bokassa, ruler of the Central African Republic.

Politics in Paris

Among Giscard d'Estaing's campaign promises was the reestablishment, for the first time since the crushing of the Commune in 1871, of the office of mayor of Paris. In 1977, Giscard's conservative rival Jacques Chirac gained a narrow edge over the official candidate and became the capital's first 20th-century mayor. He wasted no time in assuming control over the city council and the municipal apparatus, which the Socialist and Communist opposition denounced publicly and the mayor's own party off-the-record. The advantages to Parisians of the new mayoralty were appreciable: the city sparkled.

One of the most significant facts of the sixties and seventies was the gradual decline of the Communist Party, from thirty percent of the Parisian electorate in the years following the war to roughly twenty percent at the end of the seventies. The causes were many, not least among them the conscious policy to rid Paris of its working-class population, pushing it into the far reaches of the outer *banlieue*. (While the nation has voted overwhelmingly socialist on a number of occasions since 1977, Paris has remained solidly conservative, electing Jacques Chirac to three successive six-year terms and his handpicked successor, Jean Tibéri, to another.)

In May 1981 François Mitterand, chairman of the Socialist Party, defeated Giscard d'Estaing for the French presidency. As soon as the election results were announced, Parisians took to the streets for a victory celebration, most symbolically, at the Bastille.

Following on the heels of Mitterand's victory, legislative elections gave a coalition of Communists and Socialists a net majority in the National Assembly. The results confirmed the Communist decline—sixteen percent as compared to the Socialist's thirty-eight percent of the electorate. However, the overriding problem of unemployment remained unmanageable, and the number of jobless continued to climb. According to official statistics, it reached twelve percent of the working population, though figures were considerably higher in certain regions, including the suburbs of Paris, and among the under twenty-five population. Twenty-nine percent of families were relegated to the category "poor."

In 1984 one million people demonstrated in the streets of Paris against the government's attempt to control the curricula of Catholic schools, which had been largely subsidized by the State since 1959.

The parliamentary elections of 1986 deprived Mitterand of a majority, as the Socialist vote plunged to 31.6% of the electorate. The Communists gained 9.7% of the vote, outperformed by Jean-Marie Le Pen's National Front (9.8%), an extreme right-wing party denunciator of corruption and incompetence among the urban and national elites. This group espoused (and continues to espouse) simplistic, racist theses that damn African immigration for France's woes.

Mitterand subsequently called on Chirac, leader of the opposition, to form a government, thereby practicing what is known as "cohabitation" between the left-leaning president and a conservative prime minister. Chirac privatized a number of State banks and industries but was neither able to raise the national growth rate, nor to reduce the public debt or unemployment. He ran for president against Mitterand in 1988 and was defeated.

During the latter's second mandate, the Socialists formed three succeeding governments, including one headed by Edith Cresson, the first woman to occupy the post of prime minister. By the time of the next parliamentary elections, in 1993, the gulf between rich and poor had again widened. Further beset by a number of corruption scandals, as well as revelations about Mitterand's membership in a fascist youth organization and his Vichy past, the Socialists were no longer credible. The right won in a landslide, capturing eighty-three percent of the seats in parliament. In 1995 Jacques Chirac defeated the Socialist candidate Lionel Jospin for the presidency.

Alain Juppé, Chirac's prime minister, was no more successful than his predecessors in resolving the economic crisis and, in 1997, the Right was defeated at the polls. The Socialists and their allies—the Communists, the Greens, and the Radicals—won a landslide victory.

The resulting Jospin "cohabitation" government with President Chirac has benefited from a significant rise in national growth. With the resolution of the economic crisis seemingly in sight and a reduction in the number of jobless, Jospin's chances of becoming the next President of France, in 2002, are substantial. Should that be the case, he would become the first Protestant to preside over the country's destiny.

Paris' second 20th-century mayor, Jean Tibéri, became the object of scandals involving election fraud and his wife's presence on the city payrolls. His defeat at the polls in March 2001 was humiliating, the overwhelmingly conservative Parisian electorate preferring a Socialist and declared homosexual, Bertrand Delanoë.

CITY LANDSCAPES

An essential motivating force set in motion by de Gaulle, and pursued by each succeeding regime, has been to ensure that Paris remains a major world economic and political capital. Despite the emphasis placed on regionalization and the implementation of policies that endow the regions with a degree of independence, the capital continues to dominate. Paris and its region represented sixteen percent of the population of France in 1946, while today it represents eighteen percent. No other European country except Austria is as top-heavy in this respect.

Furthermore, the composition of the population of Paris and its suburbs has, since the Second World War, undergone dramatic changes. In 1962, the number of foreigners residing in Paris represented eight percent of the population, the majority of which were Italian. By 1963 Algerians represented twenty percent of all foreigners living in Paris. Portuguese immigrants started arriving in the sixties, followed by Tunisians, Moroccans, and Black Africans. In the seventies, people from Vietnam and Cambodia immigrated, along with Turks, Lebanese, and Tamils.

In 1990 foreigners represented sixteen percent of the population of metropolitan Paris, half of whom are North Africans. At first glance the figures astound. However, they are no higher than 19th-century statistics, the difference being the countries of origin. Then they were all European. Grouped in the eastern and northern *arrondissements* and in outlying *cités* (housing projects) in the *banlieue*, the immigrant community suffers from unbearably high unemployment levels, and the resulting problems of poverty, crime, and drugs. Poorly educated and overwhelmingly Muslim, this population is subjected to the twin ills of racism and ostracism. Both the municipal and State administrations have made stabs at resolving the problems. As a rule, however, they have been ill-adapted or inadequately staffed and financed.

In the process of aggrandizing Paris, each president has sought to immortalize his reign. For de Gaulle, the tower was a symbol but the idea was primary. He appointed a Delegate to the District of Paris, Paul Delouvrier, who devised a strategic plan for the region that covered the creation of the *villes nouvelles*, new transportation links, and the airport that bears de Gaulle's name. Changes in the regulations governing construction were based on the eventual demolition of two out of every three Paris blocks. Luckily, de Gaulle's Minister of Culture, the writer André Malraux, had the foresight to protect the Marais district by declaring it a historic monument.

Instead of classical Paris imposing its view on the outer *arrondissements* and the suburbs, the high rises and housing projects of the latter were overtaking the city, refashioning the landscape and the skyline. This was also the period of the Montparnasse Tower, the first constructions at the Défense and the transformation of Les Halles, the old central market. In the early seventies, Parisians attacked all three projects, the general opinion being that the first had no place in traditional Paris, and that the second destructed the line of sight from the Louvre, down the Champs-Elysées, to the Arch of Triumph. As for the third, conservationists were enraged at the thought that Baltard's unique architectural treasure would be destroyed.

For Pompidou the refusal of the tower was retrograde: "Modern architecture does not exist in cities without towers!" The compromise solution for the Défense would later be the elegant Grande Arche. The Les Halles venture was complicated by the fact that no overall plan had been adopted except for the construction of an underground, central RER train station where multiple lines would converge and transfer. For years after the merchants were moved to new markets at Rungis, it remained a huge hole. Pompidou's eventual world trade center was all that was left of sweeping ideas for a modern city within the city. Giscard d'Estaing reduced these further by eliminating the trade towers, there and in general. The compromise result is the present shopping center and park, which has satisfied no one.

Another project that aroused the ire of Parisians was the proposed destruction of the Gare d'Orsay and its replacement by a luxury hotel. Pompidou was pressured into declaring the site a historic monument. Giscard subsequently approved its transformation into the outstanding 19th-century museum that it has become.

From the outset François Mitterand intended to leave his personal imprint on Paris. He began work on a series of *grands projets*, which obtained the green light from Chirac, the Gaullist mayor of Paris, whose city could only gain from the prestige. The most visible among these projects were the Grande Arche at the Défense (Johan Otto von Spreckelsen), the Science and Techniques Museum (Bernard Tschumi), and the Arab World Institute (Jean Nouvel), as well as the daring Louvre pyramid project, the Opéra Bastille, and the Library of France.

The pyramids of the new Louvre and its tremendous overhaul were the work of architect I. M. Pei, an American museum specialist who had been approached directly, there being no selection committee appointed for the project. Pei was subjected to considerable official and journalistic abuse for his modernism but, fortunately, had the full support of Mitterand who defended his choice publicly: "Basically I think I have rather classical tastes and I am attracted to pure, geometrical shapes."

The Bastille Opera, understood as the people's introduction to an art form previously reserved to the bourgeoisie, was decried upon completion for its high, "unpopular" prices. It was even dubbed a glorified Turkish bath because of its tiled exterior. Actually, its interior design is innovative, providing a great work space and allowing for simultaneous events. The Bibliothèque de France has probably been subjected to more abuse than any project since the Pompidou Center. Its four monumental glass towers, representing open books, have been criticized as unsafe for the preservation of paper, while the interior design has been judged impractical. With time, the Pompidou Center has melted into the Parisian scene. The Opera and the Library it is assumed will do the same.

Despite tensions and differences, the population of Paris displays a strong sense of belonging, of pride in their quality as Parisians. And that, as we and they realize, is a privilege.

Those who have known Paris in the past may be inclined to lament the many changes of modernization: the neighborhoods leveled and replaced by high rises, the traffic, and fast food. Whereas those glimpsing the city for the first time are still dazzled by its classic splendor. For one and all, however, its allure remains overwhelming.

INDEX

Page numbers in *italics* indicate illustrations.